IN ASSOCIATION WITH

SQA

HODDER GIBSON
Model Papers
WITH ANSWERS

PLUS: Official SQA Specimen Paper & 2015 Past Paper With Answers

Higher for CfE

Business Management

2014 Specimen Question Paper, Model Papers & 2015 Exam

HODDER
GIBSON
AN HACHETTE UK COMPANY

This book contains the official 2014 SQA Specimen Question Paper and 2015 Exam for Higher for CfE Business Management, with associated SQA approved answers modified from the official marking instructions that accompany the paper.

In addition the book contains model papers, together with answers, plus study skills advice. These papers, some of which may include a limited number of previously published SQA questions, have been specially commissioned by Hodder Gibson, and have been written by experienced senior teachers and examiners in line with the new Higher for CfE syllabus and assessment outlines, Spring 2014. This is not SQA material but has been devised to provide further practice for Higher for CfE examinations in 2015 and beyond.

Hodder Gibson is grateful to the copyright holders, as credited on the final page of the Answer Section, for permission to use their material. Every effort has been made to trace the copyright holders and to obtain their permission for the use of copyright material. Hodder Gibson will be happy to receive information allowing us to rectify any error or omission in future editions.

Hachette UK's policy is to use papers that are natural, renewable and recyclable products and made from wood grown in sustainable forests. The logging and manufacturing processes are expected to conform to the environmental regulations of the country of origin.

Orders: please contact Bookpoint Ltd, 130 Park Drive, Milton Park, Abingdon, Oxon OX14 4SE. Telephone: (44) 01235 827720. Fax: (44) 01235 400454. Lines are open 9.00–5.00, Monday to Saturday, with a 24-hour message answering service. Visit our website at www.hoddereducation.co.uk. Hodder Gibson can be contacted direct on: Tel: 0141 848 1609; Fax: 0141 889 6315; email: hoddergibson@hodder.co.uk

This collection first published in 2015 by
Hodder Gibson, an imprint of Hodder Education,
An Hachette UK Company
2a Christie Street
Paisley PA1 1NB

Typeset by Aptara, Inc.

Printed in the UK.

A catalogue record for this title is available from the British Library.

ISBN: 978-1-4718-6070-6

3 2 1

2016 2015

Introduction

Study Skills – what you need to know to pass exams!

Pause for thought

Many students might skip quickly through a page like this. After all, we all know how to revise. Do you really though?

Think about this:

"IF YOU ALWAYS DO WHAT YOU ALWAYS DO, YOU WILL ALWAYS GET WHAT YOU HAVE ALWAYS GOT."

Do you like the grades you get? Do you want to do better? If you get full marks in your assessment, then that's great! Change nothing! This section is just to help you get that little bit better than you already are.

There are two main parts to the advice on offer here. The first part highlights fairly obvious things but which are also very important. The second part makes suggestions about revision that you might not have thought about but which WILL help you.

Part 1

DOH! It's so obvious but …

Start revising in good time

Don't leave it until the last minute – this will make you panic.

Make a revision timetable that sets out work time AND play time.

Sleep and eat!

Obvious really, and very helpful. Avoid arguments or stressful things too – even games that wind you up. You need to be fit, awake and focused!

Know your place!

Make sure you know exactly **WHEN and WHERE** your exams are.

Know your enemy!

Make sure you know what to expect in the exam.

How is the paper structured?

How much time is there for each question?

What types of question are involved?

Which topics seem to come up time and time again?

Which topics are your strongest and which are your weakest?

Are all topics compulsory or are there choices?

Learn by DOING!

There is no substitute for past papers and practice papers – they are simply essential! Tackling this collection of papers and answers is exactly the right thing to be doing as your exams approach.

Part 2

People learn in different ways. Some like low light, some bright. Some like early morning, some like evening / night. Some prefer warm, some prefer cold. But everyone uses their BRAIN and the brain works when it is active. Passive learning – sitting gazing at notes – is the most INEFFICIENT way to learn anything. Below you will find tips and ideas for making your revision more effective and maybe even more enjoyable. What follows gets your brain active, and active learning works!

Activity 1 – Stop and review

Step 1

When you have done no more than 5 minutes of revision reading STOP!

Step 2

Write a heading in your own words which sums up the topic you have been revising.

Step 3

Write a summary of what you have revised in no more than two sentences. Don't fool yourself by saying, "I know it, but I cannot put it into words". That just means you don't know it well enough. If you cannot write your summary, revise that section again, knowing that you must write a summary at the end of it. Many of you will have notebooks full of blue/black ink writing. Many of the pages will not be especially attractive or memorable so try to liven them up a bit with colour as you are reviewing and rewriting. **This is a great memory aid, and memory is the most important thing.**

Activity 2 – Use technology!

Why should everything be written down? Have you thought about "mental" maps, diagrams, cartoons and colour to help you learn? And rather than write down notes, why not record your revision material?

What about having a text message revision session with friends? Keep in touch with them to find out how and what they are revising and share ideas and questions.

Why not make a video diary where you tell the camera what you are doing, what you think you have learned and what you still have to do? No one has to see or hear it, but the process of having to organise your thoughts in a formal way to explain something is a very important learning practice.

Be sure to make use of electronic files. You could begin to summarise your class notes. Your typing might be slow, but it will get faster and the typed notes will be easier to read than the scribbles in your class notes. Try to add different fonts and colours to make your work stand out. You can easily Google relevant pictures, cartoons and diagrams which you can copy and paste to make your work more attractive and **MEMORABLE**.

Activity 3 – This is it. Do this and you will know lots!

Step 1

In this task you must be very honest with yourself! Find the SQA syllabus for your subject (www.sqa.org.uk). Look at how it is broken down into main topics called MANDATORY knowledge. That means stuff you MUST know.

Step 2

BEFORE you do ANY revision on this topic, write a list of everything that you already know about the subject. It might be quite a long list but you only need to write it once. It shows you all the information that is already in your long-term memory so you know what parts you do not need to revise!

Step 3

Pick a chapter or section from your book or revision notes. Choose a fairly large section or a whole chapter to get the most out of this activity.

With a buddy, use Skype, Facetime, Twitter or any other communication you have, to play the game "If this is the answer, what is the question?". For example, if you are revising Geography and the answer you provide is "meander", your buddy would have to make up a question like "What is the word that describes a feature of a river where it flows slowly and bends often from side to side?".

Make up 10 "answers" based on the content of the chapter or section you are using. Give this to your buddy to solve while you solve theirs.

Step 4

Construct a wordsearch of at least 10 × 10 squares. You can make it as big as you like but keep it realistic. Work together with a group of friends. Many apps allow you to make wordsearch puzzles online. The words and phrases can go in any direction and phrases can be split. Your puzzle must only contain facts linked to the topic you are revising. Your task is to find 10 bits of information to hide in your puzzle, but you must not repeat information that you used in Step 3. DO NOT show where the words are. Fill up empty squares with random letters. Remember to keep a note of where your answers are hidden but do not show your friends. When you have a complete puzzle, exchange it with a friend to solve each other's puzzle.

Step 5

Now make up 10 questions (not "answers" this time) based on the same chapter used in the previous two tasks. Again, you must find NEW information that you have not yet used. Now it's getting hard to find that new information! Again, give your questions to a friend to answer.

Step 6

As you have been doing the puzzles, your brain has been actively searching for new information. Now write a NEW LIST that contains only the new information you have discovered when doing the puzzles. Your new list is the one to look at repeatedly for short bursts over the next few days. Try to remember more and more of it without looking at it. After a few days, you should be able to add words from your second list to your first list as you increase the information in your long-term memory.

FINALLY! Be inspired...

Make a list of different revision ideas and beside each one write **THINGS I HAVE** tried, **THINGS I WILL** try and **THINGS I MIGHT** try. Don't be scared of trying something new.

And remember – "FAIL TO PREPARE AND PREPARE TO FAIL!"

Higher Business Management

The practice papers

These practice papers are designed to help you prepare for the end-of-year exam by using the new course content and allowing you to become familiar with the new style of examination. The amended content and style of the examination for the new Higher means that the past papers currently available do not match the updated course.

Using these papers, along with others produced by SQA for exams or as exemplars, will give you the best opportunity to get a feel of the new exam arrangements, and so give you a much better chance of success.

The papers give you a wide range of the possible questions that you will come across in your exam, however, there will be others that are used in exams that are not included in these papers so it is important to use these in addition to all the information given on the SQA website and approved texts that are available to purchase from Hodder Gibson.

The exams

There are some important changes to the new Higher Business Management examination question paper that you should be aware of. This is especially important for you if you are going to be sitting this new Higher as one of your first experiences of the new CfE courses.

The biggest change to the examination is the move from an examination paper which contained options, to one which is now mandatory. This means that **there is no choice of questions**. The structure of the examination is outlined below.

Section one

This is based on a case study of approximately 700 words and it will include additional information in the form of exhibits (appendices). The exhibits could include financial information, graphs or charts, pictorial information, timelines etc.

This will be followed by a total of 30 marks' worth of questions. Most of the questions will relate to information contained in the case study and exhibits, and may make reference to that information. It is important that your answers to the questions relate back to the information in the case study and exhibits. There will be a maximum of around eight questions which may be split into parts. The questions can be drawn from any area of the course and will use a variety of different command words. The aim of this section of the paper is to test breadth of knowledge from any part of the course.

Section two

This section of the examination paper is made up of four questions worth 10 marks each. The 10 marks will be split into a maximum of three parts in most cases, although you may see some questions split into just two parts. The aim of this section of the paper is to test depth of knowledge and each 10-mark question will focus on one topic area of the course. The questions can be drawn from any area of the course and will use a variety of different command words.

The main topic areas of the course, which you should already know, that are available to test are:

1. Understanding business
2. Management of people
3. Management of finance
4. Management of marketing
5. Management of operations

Whilst areas 2, 3, 4 and 5 are fairly equally weighted, area 1 is large in comparison so it is fair to expect to be asked statistically more questions from this area of the course.

Answering questions in Higher Business Management

Read the question carefully

It is often easy to assume you know what you are being asked in a question by picking out a few keywords. You will be in a high-pressure situation whether you think you are or not, and it's easy to try and get through the paper quickly. Take the time you need to read the question carefully. It is essential that you answer the question being asked in order to maximise the number of marks that you can access. No question is deliberately worded to catch you out, or be a test of English, but you do need to understand how and why command words are used.

For example, "Describe the role of managers in staff appraisals" caused problems for many candidates as they either described the role of the manager or staff appraisals. This did not answer the question and so they could not be given marks. The role of manager had to be *related* to staff appraisals in order to answer the question fully and correctly.

Answering the command words

Each question in Higher for CfE Business Management has a command word to help you understand what is needed in your response. Some of the most common command words used are listed below with an explanation of what is required in your response. This list is not exhaustive and other command words could be used. Typically, in the Higher Business Management examination papers, "describe" is the most commonly used command, while the command which causes candidates the most problems (possibly because it demands more knowledge and application of that knowledge) is "explain".

Commonly used command words in Higher for CfE Business Management

Identify is the most straightforward command word, and a short answer is all that is required. For example, "Identify a source of finance for a business".

The answer could be as simple as "A loan from a bank". However, there will be few identify marks available at Higher level so don't count on being able to give many short answers.

Describe requires a more detailed answer, giving the main features. It must be a description of something. Additional marks may be available if you give examples in, or further depth to, your description. These are sometimes referred to as development points.

For example, "A loan from a bank which is repaid over time in equal instalments with interest".

Outline is similar to describe but can be worded in such a way that a more detailed answer is actually required.

For example, "Outline the impact on a business if banks raise interest rates".

To get the mark, you would need to write more than "They would have to make higher payments on bank loans". You would have to add "which will increase costs to the business, which may lower profits" to show the impact.

However, if you were to answer a question such as, "Outline the main stages of the recruitment process", the answer required could simply be a list.

Discuss normally requires you to give advantages and disadvantages, or both sides of an argument. It is not always necessary to give both sides of the debate to be awarded full marks, provided that your points are fully developed.

For example, "Discuss the use of bank loans for a business".

Answers could include: "Allows the business to spread repayments over a longer period of time", "Which will help with cash flow" and "The business will have to pay interest on the money borrowed".

Distinguish requires you to list the differences between two things. It is important to understand that you only get **one mark** for each distinguishing point.

For example, "Distinguish between a bank loan and a mortgage".

To answer this question you need to say what the differences are: "A bank loan is normally for a short period such as 5 years, whereas a mortgage is for a much longer period such as 30 years". Note that this discussion point would be worth only one mark.

Compare is similar in some ways to distinguish, but also allows you to write what is similar as well as what the differences are.

For example, "Compare a bank loan and a mortgage".

Answers could include the distinguishing point above, but also similarities such as "Both are repaid with added interest".

Explain requires a more detailed answer. Essentially it can be thought of as a description plus an explanation of why something is the way it is.

For example, "Explain the disadvantages of a bank loan for a business".

Your answer would need to be developed, such as, "Added interest would need to be repaid which would adversely affect the costs to the business". Added interest on its own would not gain a mark as it does not actually explain why the bank loan is a disadvantage for the business.

Good luck!

Remember that the rewards for passing Higher Business Management are well worth it! Your pass will help you get the future you want for yourself. In the exam, be confident in your own ability. If you're not sure how to answer a question, trust your instincts and just give it a go anyway.

Keep calm and don't panic! GOOD LUCK!

2014 Specimen Question Paper

National
Qualifications
SPECIMEN ONLY

SQ05/H/01

Business Management

Date — Not applicable

Duration — 2 hours and 15 minutes

Total marks — 70

SECTION 1 — 30 marks

Attempt ALL questions.

SECTION 2 — 40 marks

Attempt ALL questions.

Write your answers clearly in the answer booklet provided. In the answer booklet, you must clearly identify the question number you are attempting.

Use **blue** or **black** ink.

It is recommended that you spend 15 minutes reading over the information provided in **SECTION 1** before responding to the questions.

Before leaving the examination room you must give your answer booklet to the Invigilator; if you do not, you may lose all the marks for this paper.

SECTION 1 — 30 marks

Read ALL the following information and attempt ALL the questions that follow.

The following information has been taken from an Annual Report of J Sainsbury plc and is presented as a report to its shareholders.

J Sainsbury plc

Annual Report to shareholders 2013

The Board is pleased to report on another good year for Sainsbury's. Profits have improved and we are continuing to invest significantly in strengthening the business for the future.

Business review

A winning team

We would like to thank our 157,000 colleagues for their efforts in providing excellent customer service. Our people are the face of Sainsbury's and are central to our success. We continue to invest in their training and development, and in ensuring Sainsbury's is a great place to work. Many of our colleagues have benefited from externally certified training qualifications in our seven food colleges. We are delighted that they share in a record bonus of over £90 million this year.

Sainsbury's Bank

Whilst our core business remains supermarkets, the move into banking with Lloyds Banking Group in 1997 has proved profitable. We have now reached an agreement to acquire Lloyds' 50 per cent shareholding and take full ownership of Sainsbury's Bank.

Our values

Our unique values and strong corporate culture are at the heart of our success and this remains as true today as it was when we were founded 144 years ago. Through our ambitious *20 × 20 Sustainability Plan* we aim to:

- *Source raw materials with integrity* — by ensuring our products ensure sustainability, eg responsibly caught seafood and no contribution to global deforestation
- *Reduce consumption of unhealthy foods* — by providing clear nutritional information
- *Respect our environment* — by reducing carbon emissions and continuing to use solar energy
- *Be a great place to work* — by providing certificated training for employees
- *Make a positive difference to the community* — by encouraging children to enjoy physical activity

Loyalty and insight

Nearly 12 million Sainsbury's customers regularly use their loyalty card and the data gathered from these cards enables us to understand our customers better and offer them targeted promotions.

Market overview

The UK economic climate in 2012/13 continued to be challenging. Inflation outstripped wage growth, squeezing household budgets. However, consumer confidence is improving due to continued low interest rates and falling unemployment.

Although the outlook has improved slightly over the year, consumer confidence is still lower than it was five years ago due to rising living costs and changes to taxation and benefits. People are buying slightly less in their weekly grocery shop and then topping it up locally in convenience stores.

SECTION 1 (continued)

Customers are more price-conscious than ever, looking for discounts and offers to help them save money. Despite the economic downturn, consumers are still willing to spend money on expensive ethical products such as fair trade items. People carefully consider their spending decisions and have greater expectations of the quality and integrity of goods and services they buy.

Strategy for growth

The following five-point plan highlights our strategy going forward:

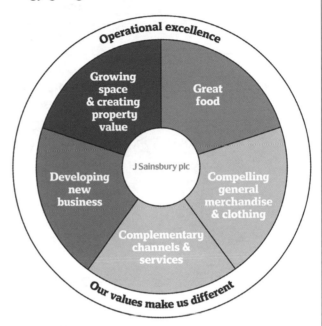

- *Great food* — the quality and value of our food, combined with our strong ethical standards and supplier relationships, differentiate us from other supermarkets and help our customers to *Live Well for Less*.

- *Compelling general merchandise and clothing* — *Tu* is the seventh most popular clothing brand in the UK and we sell more bakeware than our rivals.

- *Complementary channels of distribution and services* — we offer a winning mix of supermarkets, convenience stores and an online service.

- *Developing new business* — we continue our drive into the online and digital entertainment market with the purchase of a majority stake in Anobii, now operating as *eBooks by Sainsbury's*. Sainsbury's pharmacies are now open in over 270 stores and in three hospitals. We are finding other new ways to offer our services — from our online retail website to our innovative *Mobile Scan & Go*.

- *Growing space and creating property value* — we are increasing our store portfolio by adding bright, modern extensions, and state-of-the-art new supermarkets and convenience stores.

Source: Adapted from J Sainsbury plc Annual Report 2013

Further information

Exhibit 1 — Extract from Sainsbury's financial performance

	2012/13	2011/12	Change
	£ millions	£ millions	%
Sales	23,303	22,294	+ 4·5
Gross Profit	829	789	+ 5·1
Net Profit	614	598	+ 2.7

Source: Adapted from J Sainsbury plc Annual Report 2013

Exhibit 2 — Sainsbury's market share

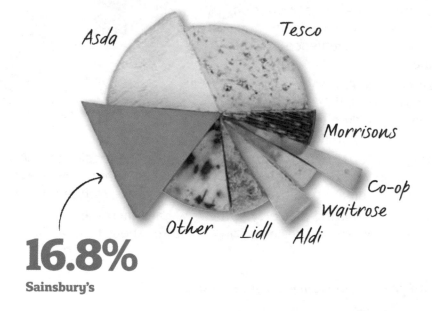

Source: Kantar Worldpanel total till roll for the 52 weeks to 17 March 2013

Exhibit 3 — Sainsbury's growth timeline

1869	First store opened on London's Drury Lane
1950s	First self-service stores opened
1970s	Introduced the first bakeries, fresh fish counters, coffee shops and petrol stations
1994	First major supermarket in the UK to sell fair trade food
1996	Began recycling partnership with Oxfam
1997	Started Sainsbury's Bank in a joint venture with Lloyds Banking Group
2004	Launched the *Tu* fashion range
2009	First major retailer to stop selling eggs from caged hens
2010	Opened the first of our seven food colleges — with over 20,000 colleagues given off-the-job training
2012	Sainsbury's was the only sponsor for the 2012 Paralympic Games and was a major partner of the Diamond Jubilee celebrations Purchased majority stake in e-book business Anobii

Source: Adapted from J Sainsbury plc Annual Report 2013

MARKS

The following questions are based on ALL the information provided and on knowledge and understanding you have gained whilst studying the Course.

1. (a) (i) Describe what is meant by market share. 1

   (ii) Describe People, Process and Physical Evidence used by Sainsbury's in the information provided. 3

   (b) Discuss the methods of growth used by Sainsbury's in the information provided. 6

   (c) Describe, using evidence from the information provided, ethical and environmental factors Sainsbury's has taken into account. 5

   (d) Describe the profitability ratios used to analyse financial data. 3

   (e) Explain the impact on Sainsbury's of the external factors highlighted in the information provided. 6

   (f) Compare Sainsbury's method of staff training with on-the-job training. 4

   (g) Describe the interdependence of Sainsbury's stakeholders identified in the information provided. 2

MARKS

SECTION 2 — 40 marks
Attempt ALL questions

1. (a) Describe the selection methods used to appoint new employees.   4

    (b) Explain the benefits of using information technology to deliver staff training.   3

    (c) Describe one theory of motivation used by managers.   3

2. (a) Describe the reasons a profitable organisation may experience cashflow problems.   4

    (b) Discuss the advantages and disadvantages of using ratio analysis.   6

3. (a) Describe the production methods an organisation could use.   4

    (b) Discuss the use of a just-in-time stock control system.   6

4. (a) Describe the benefits of maintaining a product portfolio.   4

    (b) Compare the use of penetration pricing with skimming pricing.   3

    (c) Describe into the pipeline promotions that an organisation could use.   3

[END OF SPECIMEN QUESTION PAPER]

Model Paper 1

Whilst this Model Paper has been specially commissioned by Hodder Gibson for use as practice for the Higher (for Curriculum for Excellence) exams, the key reference documents remain the SQA Specimen Paper 2014 and SQA Past Paper 2015.

National
Qualifications
MODEL PAPER 1

Business Management

Duration — 2 hours and 15 minutes

Total marks — 70

SECTION 1 — 30 marks

Attempt ALL questions.

SECTION 2 — 40 marks

Attempt ALL questions.

Write your answers clearly in the answer booklet provided. In the answer booklet, you must clearly identify the question number you are attempting.

Use **blue** or **black** ink.

It is recommended that you spend 15 minutes reading over the information provided in **SECTION 1** before responding to the questions.

Before leaving the examination room you must give your answer booklet to the Invigilator; if you do not, you may lose all the marks for this paper.

SECTION 1 — 30 marks

Read ALL the following information and attempt ALL the questions that follow.

The following information has been taken from a newspaper report on changes to the Wonga image.

Cuddly grandparent puppets axed as Wonga attempts big clean-up

Wonga.com is the trading name of WDFC UK Ltd offering short-term loans that banks don't. After its regular appearances in the media as the example for all that is bad in payday lending, Wonga is attempting to offer a new image to customers and its critics.

Andy Haste, the former chief executive of the insurance giant RSA, is to become chairman of the company and his first job will be to announce a review of how the business currently operates.

This review is intended to clean up Wonga's advertising and Mr Haste stated that the Wonga grandparent puppets will go. He said Wonga did not want to be associated with "anything which inadvertently attracts children". Mr Haste will also look at stopping advertising during children's programmes as part of the review. The payday loan sector as a whole has been criticised for advertising during children's programmes. Ofcom, the government approved regulator for broadcasting and competition, is already looking at the situation.

Respectability for Wonga

Mr Haste says he wants to change the image, even if it means it will make less money. "Our goal is to deliver the original vision for Wonga — to provide short-term lending to the right customers in a responsible and transparent way" he said, adding: "... we will become a more customer focused, and inevitably in the near term, a smaller and less profitable business."

"However, we are determined to make the necessary changes and serve our customers in the right way, to repair our reputation and become a business with a long-term future and an accepted place in the financial services industry."

Wonga has faced its fair share of criticism — not least the recent revelation that it sent out fake legal letters to its own customers who were having problems repaying loans.

Whether this process being introduced by Mr Haste will gain them more trust from their customers or politicians remains to be seen. But, for Mr Haste, at least, this is the start of a programme he hopes will make Wonga respectable.

SECTION 1 (continued)

Financial Conduct Authority (FCA)

People using payday lenders will see the cost of borrowing fall significantly from next year. The financial regulator (FCA) has imposed a cap on payday lending which means no one will have to pay back more than twice the amount they borrowed.   Last year around one and a half million people took out payday loans.

"Payday Loan" rates should be capped said the Financial Conduct Authority (FCA), and in total, no one will have to pay back more than twice what they borrowed.   The payday industry said the changes, due in January 2015, will mean more people turning to loan sharks.

There will also be a cap on missed payment charges. "For the many people that struggle to repay their payday loans every year, this is a giant leap forward" said FCA chief executive Martin Wheatley.

The FCA estimates that payday lenders will lose £420 million a year as a result of the changes or 42% of their revenue but it says consumers will save an average of £193 each a year.   FCA chief Martin Wheatley said: "Many payday loans companies will go out of business." Wonga currently charges £37.15 to borrow £100 for a month, while The Money Shop charges £29.99. Both would have to cut these fees to £24.

Church of England investment withdrawn

The Archbishop of Canterbury, the Most Reverend Justin Welby, Head of the Church of England, has said he is "absolutely delighted" that the Church has ended its investment in the payday lender Wonga.

The move ends an embarrassing situation for the Church, who last year pledged to try to put Wonga out of business by helping other small lenders compete with it.   It later emerged that the Church had indirectly staked about £75,000 in Wonga through an investment fund.

Sources: http://www.bbc.co.uk/news/business-28294258
http://www.bbc.co.uk/news/business-28305886
http://www.bbc.co.uk/news/business-28260222

SECTION 1 (continued)

Further information

Exhibit 1 — Statistics from Wonga

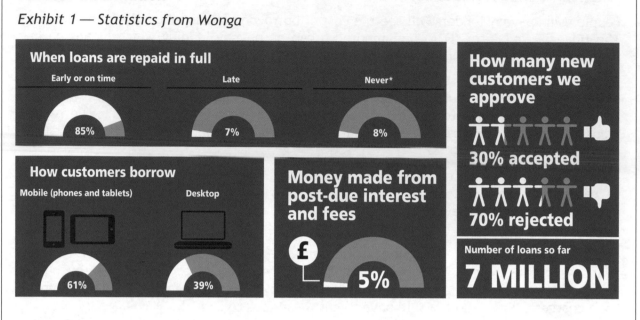

Exhibit 2 — The Wonga review's six key areas

- Strengthening affordability for customers
- Tightening lending criteria
- Address the total cost of credit and ensure even greater transparency in Wonga's products
- Advertising and not appealing to the young
- A technology overhaul
- Working more closely with regulators

Exhibit 3 — The measure announced by the FCA includes:

- Initial cap of 0.8% a day in interest charges. Someone who takes out a loan of £100 over 30 days, and pays back on time, will therefore pay no more than £24 in interest.
- Default fees capped at £15. Borrowers who fail to pay back on time can be charged a maximum of £15, plus 0.8% a day in outstanding interest.
- Total cost cap of 100%. Even if a borrower defaults, he or she will never have to pay back more than twice the amount they borrowed.

Sources: http://www.openwonga.com/ (last accessed 17/05/2015)
http://www.bbc.co.uk/news/business-28294258
http://www.bbc.co.uk/news/business-28305886

MARKS

The following questions are based on ALL the information provided and on knowledge and understanding you have gained whilst studying the Course.

1. (a) Describe the features of the type of organisation Wonga operates as.   4

    (b) Describe the consequences for Wonga if it fails to operate responsibly in the future.   3

    (c) (i) Justify the advertising decisions planned by Mr Haste in the case study.   2

         (ii) Describe the role of Ofcom as an external political factor.   3

    (d) Describe the ratios that Wonga could use to measure the impact of the changes made by the Financial Conduct Authority.   6

    (e) Explain the benefits of staff training in helping Wonga implement the proposed changes.   4

    (f) Describe the technology that will allow Wonga to increase sales.   3

    (g) Discuss the conflict of interest between Wonga owners and the following stakeholders:

         • Financial Conduct Authority

         • Customers

         • Church of England.   5

MARKS

SECTION 2 — 40 marks

Attempt ALL questions

1. (a) Describe the sources of finance available to a public limited company.   4

   (b) Describe the purpose of an income statement (trading, profit and loss account).   3

   (c) Explain the use of cash budgets.   3

2. (a) Explain the change in profits during the product life cycle.   4

   (b) Discuss the pricing strategies an organisation could use.   4

   (c) Describe the changes in retailing in recent years.   2

3. (a) Describe the quality methods that an organisation may use.   6

   (b) Discuss the environmental issues faced by manufacturers.   4

4. (a) Distinguish between internal and external recruitment.   4

   (b) Justify the use of work-based qualifications.   2

   (c) Describe the use of appraisals.   4

[END OF MODEL PAPER]

Model Paper 2

Whilst this Model Paper has been specially commissioned by Hodder Gibson for use as practice for the Higher (for Curriculum for Excellence) exams, the key reference documents remain the SQA Specimen Paper 2014 and SQA Past Paper 2015.

HODDER GIBSON
LEARN MORE

National Qualifications
MODEL PAPER 2

Business Management

Duration — 2 hours and 15 minutes

Total marks — 70

SECTION 1 — 30 marks

Attempt ALL questions.

SECTION 2 — 40 marks

Attempt ALL questions.

Write your answers clearly in the answer booklet provided. In the answer booklet, you must clearly identify the question number you are attempting.

Use **blue** or **black** ink.

It is recommended that you spend 15 minutes reading over the information provided in **SECTION 1** before responding to the questions.

Before leaving the examination room you must give your answer booklet to the Invigilator; if you do not, you may lose all the marks for this paper.

HODDER GIBSON
LEARN MORE

SECTION 1 — 30 marks

Read ALL the following information and attempt ALL the questions that follow.

The Never Ending Evolution of Elysium Luxury Stores

A huge range of luxury brands, designer clothing and expensive homeware offered for sale in an upmarket environment doesn't seem to be enough to tempt customers to part with their cash at Elysium Luxury Stores these days. Roland Martin the Chief Executive of Elysium was forced to admit to shareholders that the brand's sales performance was simply not good enough at their recent Annual General Meeting (AGM). Many shareholders expressed their anger at the time it was taking to revive the internationally renowned luxury chain. Clothing and homeware were singled out as the worst performers despite a recent diversification of the brands on offer to customers.

Elysium reported its 8th consecutive drop in quarterly sales of merchandise, with trading hit by problems after the launch of its new website and online ordering system. Mr Martin admitted that issues with Elysium's revamped website had "a significant impact on sales" with online purchases down 5% in the latest quarter. He was, however, keen to also attribute this to a general downturn in consumer spending habits on luxury goods.

One shareholder said: "This must be the slowest turnaround in history." Another said Elysium had forgotten how to produce and stock goods "that appeal to the target market".

The new website was supposed to transform the business but has faced problems since its launch. All four million customers registered on the old site were forced to re-register and there have been reports of problems with ordering. One of the unique services offered as part of the online experience was a guarantee of next day delivery for orders placed prior to 3pm the day before. This even applied to stock held outwith the UK and many analysts had questioned the wisdom of making such a promise to high value customers.

Customers reported that the new website was difficult to use and orders were not arriving the next day as promised. One head of a digital retailing organisation stated that if you need more than three clicks to find anything, you are likely to lose the customer. Not being able to deliver on time merely added to customers' frustrations.

Problems with online sales contributed to a significant fall in like-for-like sales of general merchandise over a quarterly period. However the fall was offset by continued growth in Elysium's premium brands which increased by 2%.

The retailer said sales of fashion clothing increased during the quarter but like-for-like clothing sales overall were down by 1.3%. Mr Martin said: "We have enjoyed a continued improvement in clothing sales, although as we feared the problems of the new Elysium. com site has had an impact on sales. "We are pleased that the premium fashion clothing business has continued to grow, helped by full price sales, in line with our increased focus on margins.

SECTION 1 (continued)

"Our premium brands business had another great quarter, continuing to outperform the market, through our focus on quality and new products creating differentiation from our competitors." Brian Wilson, a senior retail analyst said: "The latest update from Elysium tells an old tale: that the strategy on high value goods will deliver results if only it is given more time and the right support for these big spend customers."

George Green, a finance analyst, said: "Against a backdrop of low expectation, Elysium appears to have offered some hope for future growth." For now, Elysium remains a work in progress. The group's offering continues to be developed, premium goods sales are expanding, bolstered by the roll-out of new franchised brand stores, whilst the strength of the group's brand name and the still attractive dividend yield cannot be forgotten."

Earlier this year Elysium announced plans to open 50 stores abroad and increase international profits by 30% over the next three years. The UK-based retailer is planning to open stores in markets such as France, Spain, Poland, and the lucrative Middle East. The expansion includes 20 premium brand outlets in Paris and lingerie and beauty stores in the Middle East and Spain. The new expansion move will see a "bricks and clicks" approach, with flagship stores backed by an online service at home and in store.

Plans for the future

Elysium's expansion will continue with the opening of 15 new UK stores in its franchising operations over the next few years. The priority remains in delivering quality and innovations to its customers to ensure, as a premium retailer, it offers exciting new products from top designer brands.

It will continue to invest heavily in its target markets, but the use of franchising will allow it to expand with low risk and high impact on the high street. It will also expand its premium brand stores internationally where markers can be identified, particularly in Europe, targeting wealthy areas such as Monaco and the south of France.

SECTION 1 (continued)

Further information

Exhibit 1 — Elysium.com: facts at a glance

Sales £700m up 15% for the year	Weekly website visits 4.3m up 5.6%	Mobile and tablet sales increase 87%	Premium brand stores 342 up by 26

"With our new exciting website now fully operational, our customers can now enjoy anytime access to our full range of products. Responding to our customers' changing expectations, we are bringing together the best of our in-store and online shopping experiences. Combining them allows us to offer our customers the full range of products at all of our high street branches."

Exhibit 2 — Key statistics

Group revenue	£7.8 billion
General Merchandise revenue	£3.9 billion
Premium brand revenue	£5.6 billion
UK stores	122
International revenue	£0.9 billion
International stores	204
International territories	18

Exhibit 3 — The Gamma Plan: Mission Statement

The Gamma Plan sets out our long term strategy to become a environmentally sustainable, multichannel retailer on the world stage. It will drive how we operate and develop the business for years to come.

Inspired — aim to excite and inspire our customers

Listening — listen actively and act thoughtfully

Integrity — always work to do the right thing

Innovate — aim to improve things for the better for all our stakeholders

Honesty — aim to work in an ethical and honest way with all our stakeholders

MARKS

The following questions are based on ALL the information provided and on knowledge and understanding you have gained whilst studying the Course.

1. (a) Discuss the advantages and disadvantages of the technology used by Elysium in the case study.

    6

    (b) Justify the value of a mission statement, such as Exhibit 3, on Elysium's website.

    2

    (c) From the case study, explain the conflict of interest of Elysium's stakeholders.

    4

    (d) (i) Describe the advantages and disadvantages of expanding Elysium outlets in the Middle East.

    5

    (ii) Describe the sources of finance which Elysium could use to fund its expansion overseas.

    4

    (e) Explain the benefits of franchising for Elysium.

    3

    (f) Describe the impact of current employment legislation on Elysium.

    4

    (g) Compare the features of two types of decision made by Elysium.

    2

MARKS

SECTION 2 — 40 marks
Attempt ALL questions

1. (a) Describe the benefits of stocking Fair Trade goods. 2

   (b) Compare job and batch production. 4

   (c) Discuss the use of quality circles. 4

2. (a) Describe the possible impact of liquidity problems for a business. 3

   (b) Describe the methods of improving liquidity. 4

   (c) Justify the use of spreadsheet software for preparing annual accounts. 3

3. (a) Discuss the methods of external recruitment. 4

   (b) Describe the impact on motivation of different types of leadership. 3

   (c) Describe the role of ACAS in employee relations. 3

4. (a) Describe the benefits of market research. 2

   (b) Explain the extension strategies used for a product. 4

   (c) Discuss the role of the wholesaler. 4

[END OF MODEL PAPER]

Model Paper 3

Whilst this Model Paper has been specially commissioned by Hodder Gibson for use as practice for the Higher (for Curriculum for Excellence) exams, the key reference documents remain the SQA Specimen Paper 2014 and SQA Past Paper 2015.

HODDER
GIBSON
LEARN MORE

National Qualifications
MODEL PAPER 3

Business Management

Duration — 2 hours and 15 minutes

Total marks — 70

SECTION 1 — 30 marks
Attempt ALL questions.

SECTION 2 — 40 marks
Attempt ALL questions.

Write your answers clearly in the answer booklet provided. In the answer booklet, you must clearly identify the question number you are attempting.

Use **blue** or **black** ink.

It is recommended that you spend 15 minutes reading over the information provided in **SECTION 1** before responding to the questions.

Before leaving the examination room you must give your answer booklet to the Invigilator; if you do not, you may lose all the marks for this paper.

SECTION 1 — 30 marks

Read ALL the following information and attempt ALL the questions that follow.

The following information has been taken from the Mary's Meals website.

Mary's Meals

Mary's Meals is a charity that works to support a school feeding programme for over 920,000 children across the world. It all started in 1992 when two brothers, Magnus and Fergus MacFarlane-Barrow, were watching the television news coverage of the Bosnian conflict. They started an appeal for food and blankets and filled a Jeep and drove to Bosnia. When they returned and went back to work, they discovered that donations were still arriving. Magnus gave up his job for a year and kept making trips to Bosnia with donations. The donations didn't stop and Magnus set up a charity, Scottish International Relief, which expanded its work into Romania, Liberia and Croatia. By 2002, the charity was supporting a famine relief project in Malawi. As Magnus helped support the children of a mother who was dying of AIDS, the inspiration for Mary's Meals was born: to provide chronically hungry children with one meal every school day. This helps to encourage children to gain education and lift them out of poverty. By 2014, the charity now known as Mary's Meals was providing meals to children in Africa, Asia, the Caribbean, Eastern Europe and South America.

A simple solution to world hunger

For many children, Mary's Meals may be the only meal they will have in a day. In Malawi, it costs £8.20 to provide Mary's Meals to one child for a whole school year and an average of £12.20 per child per year globally. The meals are made using locally produced food wherever possible. This respects local culture and tastes and avoids transport costs.

The charity also works in partnership with local communities wherever possible. In Malawi, over 60,000 volunteers cook and serve over 600,000 meals every school day.

Mary's Meals aims to spend at least 93p of every £1 that is donated to carry out charitable work. It does this by making extensive use of volunteers and by monitoring and controlling costs to keep them as low as possible.

It works with other partner organisations and supports other charitable work. (See Exhibit 1 and Exhibit 3 for more information.)

Ethical and morally responsible business practice

Mary's Meals can be seen to be an ethical business model. It exists to provide a service to people using resources that have been donated by other people. The Mary's Meals vision is that every child receives one daily meal in their place of education, and that all those who have more than they need share with those who lack even the most basic things.

The mission of the charity is to enable people to offer their money, goods, skills, time, or prayer, and through this involvement, providing the most effective help to those suffering the effects of extreme poverty in the world's poorest communities.

SECTION 1 (continued)

Donations

Mary's Meals is dependent on donations of money in order to operate. The Mary's Meals website is available in different languages and you can make a donation online. It is also possible to make a regular donation to the charity from your bank account or donate by phone, by text or by post. Some people may choose to keep a donation box in their home and encourage visitors who come for dinner to make a donation to Mary's Meals.

Counting on support from around the globe, Mary's Meals has fundraising entities and registered charity arms in Austria, Canada, Croatia, France, Germany, Italy, Ireland, the Netherlands, Portugal, Spain, the United Kingdom and the USA. It promotes the fact that a maximum of 7p in every £1 donated is used for corporate governance.

(Further information is available in Exhibit 2 and Exhibit 3.)

Source: http://www.marysmeals.org.uk

SECTION 1 (continued)

Further information

Exhibit 1 — Mary's Meals projects and partnership working

Use of celebrities	Celebrities help raise the profile of the work of the charity, eg Hollywood star Gerard Butler recently visited Mary's Meals in Liberia
The backpack project	Over 420,000 donated backpacks have been sent overseas to help children attending school
Saving Grace	A short animation telling the story of 10-year-old Grace
Sponsor a school	Rather than making a donation to the charity, people or groups are encouraged to sponsor an entire school
Stage a screening of Child 31	A film made to raise awareness of the work of Mary's Meals

Exhibit 2 — Key statistics

Mary's Meals Charity

		Unrestricted funds £	Restricted funds £	2013 Total £	2012 Total £
Incoming resources					
Incoming resources from generated funds:					
Voluntary income	2	8,043,912	3,837,541	11,881,453	7,755,910
Activities for generating funds	3	559,809	–	559,809	1,893,901
Investment income		11,801	–	11,801	8,839
Incoming resources from charitable activities		917	–	917	360
Tax reclaimed on Gift Aid		452,315	16,000	468,315	334,666
Total incoming resources		9,068,754	3,853,541	12,922,295	9,993,676

SECTION 1 (continued)

Exhibit 3 — Facts at a glance

- Total number of children receiving a daily meal in school = 894,288

- Average global cost of Mary's Meals per child, per year = £12.20

- Worldwide average cost per meal = 6 pence

- Number of chronically hungry children in the world = 300 million (around 57 million of these children are out of school)

- Number of backpacks sent overseas in 2014 (so far) = 20,872

- Total number of backpacks delivered to date = 402,680

- In addition to school feeding projects, Mary's Meals supports a children's home project in Romania

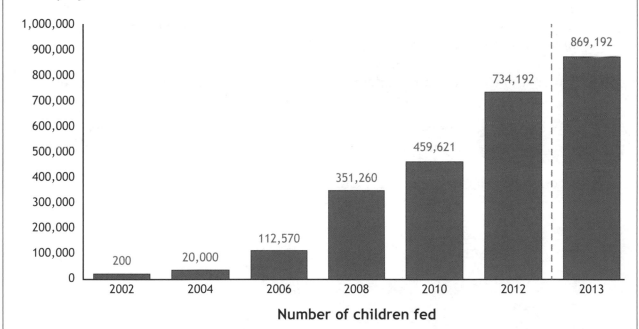

Number of children fed

Exhibit 4 — How money is spent

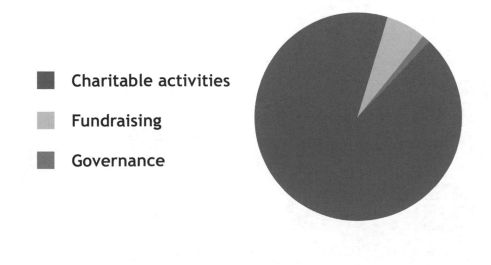

■ **Charitable activities**

▪ **Fundraising**

■ **Governance**

MARKS

The following questions are based on ALL the information provided and on knowledge and understanding you have gained whilst studying the Course.

1. (a) Using the case study, compare the objectives of Mary's Meals to a public sector organisation.   3

    (b) Discuss the potential areas of conflict for Mary's Meals as it mostly operates in overseas countries.   5

    (c) Describe the promotional strategies used by Mary's Meals to attract donations.   5

    (d) Explain the importance for Mary's Meals to operate as an ethically responsible business.   3

    (e) Describe the market research methods that Mary's Meals could use to gather information from its donors.   6

    (f)   (i) With reference to the information in Exhibit 2, suggest the reasons for an increase in voluntary income in 2013.   2

         (ii) Distinguish between two sources of finance which Mary's Meals could use to further expand.   2

    (g) Describe the impact of internal factors on a charity like Mary's Meals.   4

MARKS

SECTION 2 — 40 marks

Attempt ALL questions

1. (a) Describe the benefits of staff training.   5

   (b) Compare autocratic and laissez-faire styles of leadership.   3

   (c) Justify the use of appraisals as a tool to make decisions on employee pay.   2

2. (a) Describe the use of the following ratios:
   - profitability
   - liquidity
   - efficiency.   6

   (b) Describe the use of cash budgeting for planning.   4

3. (a) Describe the methods of reducing waste.   3

   (b) Explain the advantages of using just-in-time stock control.   3

   (c) Discuss the advantages and disadvantages of using the rail network to distribute stock.   4

4. (a) Outline the advantages of a tall organisation structure.   3

   (b) Describe how the objective of profit maximisation could negatively impact on employees in an organisation.   3

   (c) Discuss the importance of having a positive corporate culture.   4

[END OF MODEL PAPER]

Model Paper 4

Whilst this Model Paper has been specially commissioned by Hodder Gibson for use as practice for the Higher (for Curriculum for Excellence) exams, the key reference documents remain the SQA Specimen Paper 2014 and SQA Past Paper 2015.

HODDER
GIBSON
LEARN MORE

National Qualifications
MODEL PAPER 4

Business Management

Duration — 2 hours and 15 minutes

Total marks — 70

SECTION 1 — 30 marks
Attempt ALL questions.

SECTION 2 — 40 marks
Attempt ALL questions.

Write your answers clearly in the answer booklet provided. In the answer booklet, you must clearly identify the question number you are attempting.

Use **blue** or **black** ink.

It is recommended that you spend 15 minutes reading over the information provided in **SECTION 1** before responding to the questions.

Before leaving the examination room you must give your answer booklet to the Invigilator; if you do not, you may lose all the marks for this paper.

SECTION 1 — 30 marks

Read ALL the following information and attempt ALL the questions that follow.

The following information has been taken from the Arnold Clark website.

Arnold Clark

Arnold Clark is Europe's leading independently owned family-run car dealer. The business was established in 1954 by Sir Arnold Clark who still presides over the organisation as Chairman and Chief Executive. The company has grown to cover the whole of the UK with over 200 branches incorporating 130 service

centres, 40 accident repair centres and 13 parts centres. Over 15,000 new and used cars are held in stock and you can choose a new car from any of the 24 different manufacturers available. The company has a database of some 2 million customers across the UK and has diversified over the years to also offer business leasing and fleet services, car finance, car insurance and accident management amongst other services.

Other facts and figures are available in Exhibit 1 and Exhibit 3.

Corporate Social Responsibility

Arnold Clark is involved in many activities where it strives to improve the communities in which it operates. This includes charity and sponsorship of schools, football teams, hospices and athletes to name but a few. It also operates an annual artwork schools' challenge which is hotly contested each year. The business has on-going links with The Prince's Trust Scotland and the Energy Saving Trust. This also provides excellent opportunities for advertising and promotion as well as promoting positive corporate responsibility.

Investment in staff

Arnold Clark purchased GTG Training in 2003 and now has state-of-the-art training facilities in Glasgow, Edinburgh and Wolverhampton. GTG Training provides top quality training and education in areas such as business, computers and IT, health and safety, transport and automotive technical.

GTG also provides training services to many of the UK's largest companies, including Arnold Clark Automobiles Ltd, major banks, public utilities, emergency services, the NHS and many local authorities.

Growth by acquisition

Although Sir Arnold Clark started business in 1954 in Glasgow with a single car showroom, the business has grown and developed over several decades. During the 1960s, the business started to grow after buying three other garages. In addition, the car finance section of the business started up followed by the rental facility shortly after.

SECTION 1 (continued)

In 1966 the organisation won its first contract hire business and supplied 30 vehicles. 1968 saw a further development with the opening of the accident repair centre. During the 1970s and 1980s, there was continued and rapid expansion of the business as it acquired more dealerships and took over other businesses. In the 1990s, the first super-site was developed on the site of the defunct car production plant at Linwood near Glasgow Airport.

In 1993 the business ventured into new territory with the start up of Arnold Clark insurance services covering motoring, household and travel insurance. 1994 was an important year as it marked the first dealership to open in England. This was in Liverpool and more car showrooms followed both in Scotland and England.

During the 2000s, the business has continued to expand and diversify. *Further financial information is available in Exhibit 1 and Exhibit 2.*

Customer satisfaction

2014 sees the 60-year anniversary of Arnold Clark starting out in business. With over two million customers and a satisfaction rate of 94%, the business firmly believes that the reasons for its success include:

- **Huge choice of cars**

- **Superb value** — 72% of Arnold Clark customers save money when changing their car and 76% of customers have improved their MPG.

- **Fantastic service** — a massive 97% of Arnold Clark customers would recommend us to their friends and family.

- **Customer loyalty**

- **Long history**

- **Wide coverage**

- **Award-winning website** — with more than 60,000 visitors to ArnoldClark.com every day.

- **Motoring peace of mind** — ACCIST, a free accident management service, comes as standard with every vehicle.

- **Quality** — Every car goes through a 120-point inspection before being sold.

Source: http://www.arnoldclark.com

SECTION 1 (continued)

Further information

Exhibit 1 — Business structure

```
                         Arnold Clark
                      Automobiles Limited

  Arnold Clark      Arnold Clark      Arnold Clark Malta    GTG Training    Harry Fairbairn
  Finance Limited   Insurance Services   Limited            Limited         Limited
                    Limited

                           Arnold Clark      Arnold Clark
                           Insurance         Life Insurance
                           (Malta) Limited   (Malta) Limited
```

Exhibit 2 — Financial highlights

	2011	*2012*
Turnover	£2.25 billion	£2.48 billion
Pre-tax profits	£51.7 million	£60.5 million
New cars sold	72,538	79,979
Used cars sold	116,994	122,398

Exhibit 3 — Facts at a glance

- Retailer of the year in 2012, 2013 and 2014
- Established in 1954
- Over 200 dealerships across the UK
- Retailer of 24 different car brands
- Over 15,000 cars in stock
- Expansion over several decades by acquisition and organic growth
- Diversified into business leasing, car and van rental, fleet services, car finance, car insurance, household insurance, travel insurance, vehicle aftercare, servicing, MOTs, accident repairs and accident management

MARKS

The following questions are based on ALL the information provided and on knowledge and understanding you have gained whilst studying the Course.

1. (a) Using the case study, describe the benefits to Arnold Clark of having its own staff training facilities.   4

   (b) Discuss the methods of growth that Arnold Clark has used over the past 60 years.   6

   (c) (i) Describe the features of Arnold Clark's organisational grouping.   2

       (ii) Describe a leadership style that may have been used by Sir Arnold Clark.   2

   (d) Explain the advantages and disadvantages to Arnold Clark of having a corporate responsibility policy.   4

   (e) Justify the ways Arnold Clark achieves its high rate of customer satisfaction.   5

   (f) Explain the benefits to Arnold Clark's customers of using the company website.   2

   (g) Discuss the effect of the following on Arnold Clark:
       • competition from other garages
       • a downturn in the economy
       • an increase in the price of fuel.   5

MARKS

SECTION 2 — 40 marks
Attempt ALL questions

1. (a) Discuss the role of technology in the finance department. 4

   (b) Poppy Trading Ltd has calculated the following ratios for 2012 and 2013:

	2012	2013
Profitability	45%	41%
Liquidity	2:1	1.5:1

   Describe possible actions that Poppy Trading Ltd could take to improve these ratios for 2014. 6

2. (a) Explain the advantages to a business of having a varied product portfolio. 4

   (b) Describe the extension strategies that a business may put in place to support a poorly performing product. 4

   (c) Explain the use of a destroyer pricing strategy on the success of a product. 2

3. (a) Compare centralised and decentralised warehousing. 3

   (b) Discuss the use of automation in the manufacture of hi-tech products. 5

   (c) Describe the benefits to an organisation of using a mystery shopper to gather quality feedback. 2

4. (a) Explain the benefits to an organisation of supporting work-based qualifications. 3

   (b) Describe the methods of testing that could be used when recruiting new employees. 4

   (c) Describe the role of a trade union. 3

[END OF MODEL PAPER]

HIGHER FOR CfE

2015

H

National
Qualifications
2015

X710/76/11

Business Management

MONDAY, 11 MAY

1:00 PM – 3:15 PM

Total marks — 70

SECTION 1 — 30 marks

Attempt ALL questions.

SECTION 2 — 40 marks

Attempt ALL questions.

It is recommended that you spend 15 minutes reading over the information provided in **SECTION 1** before responding to the questions.

Write your answers clearly in the answer booklet provided. In the answer booklet, you must clearly identify the question number you are attempting.

Use **blue** or **black** ink.

Before leaving the examination room you must give your answer booklet to the Invigilator; if you do not, you may lose all the marks for this paper.

SECTION 1 — 30 marks

Read ALL the following information and attempt ALL the questions that follow.

Welcome to the Google plex!

Internet giant to build futuristic headquarters

INTRODUCTION

Google plc, the internet giant, has planned a massive expansion of its Californian headquarters (HQ). The 2·5 million square foot headquarters, commonly referred to as the "Googleplex", is in the midst of an approval process. This is the first time the company has commissioned a building to be designed from scratch rather than modifying premises built by others. Google will have a building designed exactly for its own purpose and one which takes staff needs into account.

CORPORATE SOCIAL RESPONSIBILITY (CSR)

Google's HQ plans to have solar panels and charging stations for employees' electric cars or indeed Google's own "driverless" cars that transport employees around the district. A low-energy heating and cooling system will allow Google to supply 100 percent fresh air economically. Most existing buildings introduce only a small percentage of fresh air. The company also seeks to eliminate potentially harmful chemicals in building materials. Google also have their own charity called "Google.org" and one of their commitments is to encourage the use of renewable energy in the United States of America.

GOOGLE'S PRODUCT PORTFOLIO

The need for a new HQ comes as Google has grown by developing many new products. It has also acquired other technology companies over the years (see Exhibit 1). Products range from the original Google search engine to the Android mobile operating system for smartphones and tablets. Google's product portfolio can be seen in more detail in Exhibit 2.

Twin Design/shutterstock.com

CORPORATE CULTURE

Google has a very relaxed corporate culture and this has been taken into account in the planning of the building. Although employees can work from outwith the office, the new HQ has been designed to encourage employees to want to be there so that they benefit from regular communication and idea sharing. Most Google employees have flexible working hours, adding to the general feeling of wellbeing.

The design will also allow employees to meet up easily and chat. Employees can wear their own casual clothes and pedal on free bicycles or walk to informal meetings in the roof gardens or coffee shops. The Googleplex will continue to use the preferred Google colour scheme of primary colours currently used in the existing HQ and will house impressive facilities. Google's offices are well-known for their perks such as gourmet cafes, sleep pods, laptops attached to gym equipment and even pool tables and bowling alleys!

RECRUITMENT AND SELECTION

Google's new employees are called "Nooglers". It may soon face competition in employing the very best potential "Nooglers" because other technology giants are also improving their offices. These rival businesses wish to ensure that they, like Google, can attract the best talent in the competitive job market.

Google and their competitors recruit for vacancies outwith their current staff from the same pool of University graduates and the wider workforce. Apple, its main competitor, is currently building an even bigger environmentally friendly campus. Meanwhile, Facebook is trying to tempt the next generation of IT graduates by creating a "Main Street" of stores, restaurants and facilities at the centre of its headquarters.

[Turn over

Exhibit 1 — Google's timeline

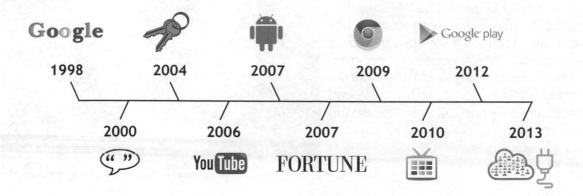

1998 — Google.com
Google.com is registered as a domain.

2000 — Google in 10 Languages
The first 10 languages of Google are released. Today, search is available in 150+ languages.

2004 — Move to new HQ
Google move to their Mountainview headquarters, 11 years before the move to their latest "Googleplex" HQ.

2006 — YouTube acquired
Google announce the takeover of YouTube.

2007 — Android
Google launch Android — the first open platform for smartphone devices.

2007 — "Fortune" Best Company to Work For
Google is rated no 1 company to work for in a well-known business magazine.

2009 — Google Chrome
Google launch their own web browser, Google Chrome.

2010 — Google TV
Google TV is launched.

2012 — Google Play
Android Market is rebranded Google Play, a digital content store offering apps, games, books, music and more.

2013 — Energy efficiency in the cloud
Google funded research shows that increased use of cloud computing would drastically reduce energy consumption.

Exhibit 2 — Google's Product Portfolio

		Market Share	
		High	Low
Market Growth	High	• Android mobile operating system • YouTube • Gmail	• Google Chrome internet browser • Google Nexus smartphone • Google TV
	Low	• Google search engine	• Google self-driving cars

Exhibit 3 — Extract from Google's financial statements for the years 2011-2013

Google plc Income Statement (Trading, Profit and Loss Account) 2011-2013

		2011 $ Million		2012 $ Million		2013 $ Million
Revenue (Sales)		$37,905		$50,175		$59,825
Less Cost of Sales		$13,188		$20,634		$25,858
GROSS PROFIT		**$24,717**		**$29,541**		**$33,967**
Less Expenses						
Sales & Advertising	$4,589		$6,143		$7,253	
Research & Development	$5,162		$6,793		$7,952	
Administration	$3,224		$3,845		$4,796	
		$12,975		$16,781		$20,001
PROFIT FOR THE YEAR (Net Profit)		**$11,742**		**$12,760**		**$13,966**

[Turn over

MARKS

The following questions are based on ALL the information provided and on knowledge and understanding you have gained whilst studying the course.

1. (a) (i) Describe the method of production used to create Google's new headquarters. **1**

   (ii) Discuss the advantages and disadvantages of the method of production described in 1(a)(i). **5**

   (b) Describe the advantages to Google of having a varied product portfolio as shown in Exhibit 2. **5**

   (c) Explain the benefits of Google's corporate culture to the organisation and its employees. **4**

   (d) As a plc, Google has to publish its final accounts as shown in Exhibit 3.

   (i) Describe the following financial terms:

   - Revenue (Sales);
   - Gross Profit. **2**

   (ii) Describe the trend in profitability using examples from Exhibit 3. **1**

   (e) Google's development of its new headquarters is an example of organic (internal) growth.

   Describe other methods of growth available to Google. **4**

   (f) Google aims to attract the best available talent from outwith its current staff.

   Discuss the use of this method of recruitment. **5**

   (g) Describe the ways in which Google demonstrates positive Corporate Social Responsibility (CSR) as shown in the case study. **3**

MARKS

SECTION 2 — 40 marks

Attempt ALL questions

2. (a) Describe the sales promotions which could be used when launching a new product.   4

    (b) Discuss the factors an organisation might consider before selecting a channel of distribution.   4

    (c) Compare the use of random sampling and quota sampling when carrying out market research.   2

3. (a) Discuss the advantages and disadvantages of centralised stock storage.   4

    (b) Explain the disadvantages of just in time stock control.   4

    (c) Describe the benefits of achieving Fairtrade certification.   2

4. (a) Describe the advantages to an organisation of using cash budgets.   4

    (b) Describe the reasons why a competitor may be interested in the financial information of an organisation.   2

    (c) Discuss the sources of long-term finance available to a plc.   4

5. (a) Describe the features of Maslow's motivation theory.   4

    (b) Explain the benefits of positive employee relations.   3

    (c) Discuss the effects of the Equality Act 2010 on an organisation.   3

[END OF QUESTION PAPER]

[BLANK PAGE]

DO NOT WRITE ON THIS PAGE

SQA AND HODDER GIBSON HIGHER FOR CfE BUSINESS MANAGEMENT 2015

HIGHER FOR CfE BUSINESS MANAGEMENT
SPECIMEN QUESTION PAPER

SECTION 1

Question			Expected Answer(s)	Max mark
1	a	i	Responses could include the following: • Market share is an organisation's percentage of the overall sales in a particular market. Accept any other suitable response.	1
		ii	Responses could include the following: **People:** anyone who comes into contact with your customers that will have an effect on customer satisfaction. • Sainsbury's ensures employees are highly trained. • Sainsbury's employees are noted for providing excellent customer service. **Process:** the ways of delivering the service, ie helpfulness of staff, quality of information given. • Providing innovative mobile scan-and-go facilities in stores. • Using e-commerce for purchases. • Using loyalty cards to maintain customer satisfaction. • Offering customers targeted promotions. • Providing nutritional information on food products. **Physical Evidence:** the tangible aspect of delivering the service, ie the building. • Providing bright and modern extensions. • Providing updated state-of-the-art stores. Accept any other suitable response.	3
1	b		Responses could include the following: Organic/internal growth • Growth of a business from its own internally generated resources (1 mark for definition). • Sainsbury's is growing by increasing the number of its state-of-the-art new supermarkets (1 mark for definition). *Advantages* • Less risky than taking over other businesses. • Can be financed through internal funds, eg retained profits. • Builds on a business's strengths, eg brands, customers. *Disadvantages* • Growth may be dependent on the growth of the overall market. • Slower method of growth — shareholders may prefer a more rapid growth. Diversification/takeover • Sainsbury's buying a majority stake in Anobii e-books (1 mark for definition). • Sainsbury's joining with Lloyds Banking Group to form Sainsbury's Bank (1 mark for definition). *Advantages (can apply to diversification or takeover)* • Reduces the risk of business failure. • Makes a larger and more financially secure business. *Disadvantages (can apply to diversification or takeover)* • Requires allocation of significant financial and human resources. • Risk of harming the main company business. Accept any other suitable response within each of the above headings.	6

Question			Expected Answer(s)	Max mark
1	c		Responses could include the following: • Suppliers' products ensure sustainability of raw materials. • Sainsbury's commitment to reducing unhealthy food and providing nutritional information. • Suppliers' products don't have a large carbon footprint (1 mark) and support renewable energies (1 development mark). • Sainsbury's commitment to making a positive difference to the communities in which it operates. • Suppliers' products are fair trade (1 mark) meaning suppliers get a fair price for products and are likely to stay in business (1 development mark). • Sainsbury's recycling partnership with Oxfam. • Suppliers ensure high standards of animal welfare. Accept any other suitable response.	5
	d		Responses could include the following: Gross profit ratio • Measures the percentage of profit that is made from buying and selling stock. Net profit ratio • Measures the percentage of profit that is made after expenses are deducted from GP. Return on capital employed • Measures the percentage of investment that is yielded as profit. Accept any other suitable response.	3
	e		Responses could include the following: • *Rising inflation* means goods/services cost more, so Sainsbury's plans to offer more great food of quality and value. • *Low interest rates* mean consumers are less likely to save and so spend more in shops like Sainsbury's (1 mark). For example, Sainsbury's sales have increased by 4·5% (1 mark for development for using Source A). • *Falling unemployment* means consumers may have more wages/disposable income to spend in shops like Sainsbury's. • *Rising living costs*, however, mean that consumers may have less disposable income to spend in Sainsbury's. • *Customers are being more price conscious* so Sainsbury's is offering more promotional offers/deals. • *Consumers are making fewer but more considered spending choices* so are buying higher quality goods such as fair trade products provided by Sainsbury's. • *Competitive factors* — Sainsbury's must be constantly aware of these, eg from Asda and Tesco, to maintain or increase its current market share of 16·8% (Exhibit 2). Accept any other suitable response.	6
	f		Responses could include the following: • Sainsbury's uses off-the-job training which takes place at training colleges away from the workplace, whereas on-the-job training takes place in the workplace. • Sainsbury's uses its own training colleges (off-the-job) which can offer intense training away from the distractions at work, whereas on-the-job training can be distracting. • When at a training college/off-the-job, the employee isn't contributing to the business, whereas with on-the-job training the employee may be doing some work. • With off-the-job training an employee learns from professional trainers/instructors/teachers, whereas with on-the-job training the employee learns from colleagues through demonstrating/coaching. • With off-the-job training the employee is away from colleagues and will still have to integrate when completed, whereas with on-the-job training, employee bonds can be built during the training process. • Sending a new employee to a training college may help them feel better prepared for the job; however, with on-the-job training the employee may feel apprehensive. • Off-the-job training is more expensive than on-the-job training. Accept any other suitable response.	4

Question			Expected Answer(s)	Max mark
1	g		Responses could include the following: • Sainsbury's (owners) need employees to operate stores and employees require Sainsbury's to provide secure jobs. • Suppliers need Sainsbury's to buy their stock and Sainsbury's needs suppliers to provide good-quality products. • Employees need customers to give money to Sainsbury's in order to have job security and customers need good-quality service from employees. • Employees need owners for wages/training/career development and owners need employees for productivity/good customer service. • Owners need customers to give them profits/market share and customers need owners for quality services/products. Accept any other suitable response.	2

SECTION 2

Question			Expected Answer(s)	Max mark
1	a		Responses could include the following: Application forms • Forms are created to request relevant information from applicants. • Comparison of applicants is easier as all provide the same information. CVs • A written summary of an applicant's experience, educational background and any other relevant information. • Candidates are free to provide the information they feel is relevant, which may not be requested on an application form. Interviews • A formal face-to-face meeting between an employer and an applicant. • Candidates can be compared in a pressure situation. • Allows candidates to respond to questions; they can also ask questions about the job/company. • Interviewers can compare notes to get a consensus on the best applicants. Assessment centres • Candidates can be observed in practical situations. • Tasks can be tailored to the vacancy, eg in-tray exercise, group task, presentation, case study. • Candidates can be moved around to work with a variety of others to see how they perform with different people and personality types. Testing • Attainment testing allows a candidate to demonstrate their skills, eg ICT, joinery skills, childcare skills. • Medical testing measures physical fitness which may be required for certain jobs, eg fire service, armed services, professional football. Accept any other suitable response.	4
	b		Responses could include the following: • Visuals from presentation software provide reinforcement to verbal information from trainer/speaker (1 mark), therefore it holds the attention of the trainees longer (1 development mark). • Staff in remote locations can be involved in training events using web conferencing, reducing the need to travel. • Live-link meetings/online tutorials can be set up between trainer and trainee so support is immediately available. • Staff being trained can access centrally-stored shared files from any geographical location. Accept any other suitable response.	3

Question			Expected Answer(s)	Max mark
1	c		Responses could include the following:	3
			Maslow's Hierarchy of Needs	
			• Maslow suggested that there were five interdependent levels of basic human needs (motivators) that must be satisfied in a strict sequence (1 mark), starting with the lowest level and working up to the highest (1 development mark).	
			• Physiological needs (to stay alive and reproduce), and security needs (to feel safe) are the most fundamental and pressing needs (1 mark).	
			• They are followed by social needs (for love and belonging), self-esteem needs (to feel worthy/ respected) and, lastly, self-actualisation needs (to realise potential and have status) (1 mark).	
			• You cannot progress to the next level in the hierarchy until the previous level is satisfied (1 mark).	
			McGregor's Theory X and Theory Y	
			• McGregor believed there were two distinct sets of assumptions that managers, in general, have about their employees (1 mark).	
			Theory-X assumptions are:	
			• Most employees dislike work and will avoid it at all costs (1 mark), therefore workers must be continually coerced, controlled and threatened to get the work done (1 development mark).	
			• Employees have little or no ambition/prefer to avoid responsibility and choose security above everything else (1 mark).	
			Theory-Y assumptions are:	
			• Most employees find work to be a source of satisfaction/are generally self-motivated in meeting individual and company goals (1 mark).	
			• Workers either seek responsibility or learn to accept it willingly (1 mark) and are motivated by the needs at the top end of Maslow's hierarchy (1 development mark).	
			Hertzberg	
			• Hertzberg believed that employee satisfaction is related to factors which motivate, and factors which cause dissatisfaction — hygiene factors (1 mark).	
			• Motivating factors give job satisfaction and include giving employees increased responsibility/ recognition for their effort/personal sense of achievement/changes for promotion, etc.	
			• Motivating factors refer to things involved in doing the job.	
			• Hygiene factors need to be met to prevent dissatisfaction and include pay and conditions/support for colleagues/company policies and procedures, etc.	
			• Hygiene factors are things which define the job.	
			Accept any other suitable response.	
2	a		Responses could include the following:	4
			• Too much money tied up in unsold stock.	
			• Customers being given too long a credit period.	
			• Customers being given too high a credit limit.	
			• Owners taking excessive cash drawings.	
			• Suppliers not allowing a trade credit period.	
			• Sudden increase in an expense, eg heat and light.	
			• High capital expenditure outlay in one month instead of spreading payments over a period of time.	
			Accept any other suitable response.	
	b		Responses could include the following:	6
			Advantages	
			• Good for comparing current performance with that of previous years.	
			• Good for comparing with rival businesses.	
			• Highlights differences in performance that will aid future decision-making/financial planning.	
			• Good for highlighting trends over a period of time.	
			Disadvantages	
			• Ratios are based on historic financial information which limits usefulness.	
			• Comparisons only useful if made with like-for-like organisations — firms in the same industry may differ in size/product mix/objectives.	
			• The accounting information used to calculate ratios does not take account of other internal factors, eg quality of managers/staff, staff motivation, staff turnover, location of business.	
			• Calculations do not show the implications of product developments or declining products.	
			• The accounting information used to calculate ratios does not include external factors — PESTEC.	
			Accept any other suitable response.	

Question			Expected Answer(s)	Max mark
3	a		Responses could include the following: • Job production — one-off single product is made to a customer's specification (1 mark). This method of production requires highly skilled workers (1 development mark) and the business can charge a premium price for the product (1 development mark). • Batch production — groups of similar products are made at the same time and no item in the batch goes to the next stage until the whole batch is ready. • Flow production — items move continuously from one operation to the next and each part of the process leads to the completion of the final product. • Labour-intensive — production is carried out by a high level of labour. • Capital-intensive — production is carried out using mainly machinery, highly automated production. Accept any other suitable response.	4
	b		Responses could include the following: • Just-in-time (JIT) stock control system reduces storage costs as stock is delivered as it is needed (1 mark). • This means that the organisation is more responsive to consumer demand (1 development mark) and that money is not tied up unnecessarily in buying large volumes of stock (1 development mark). • This can also result in less wastage of stock as it is only being ordered when it is needed (1 development mark). • However, it also means that organisations can lose out on bulk-buying discounts (1 mark). • Having a JIT system relies heavily on suppliers' co-operation in delivering stock when it is needed (1 mark). • Using a JIT system could result in high admin and delivery costs as there are many small deliveries (1 mark). • This could mean that production may be interrupted/halted if there is a delay with a delivery (1 development mark). • Deliveries of small quantities and not holding stock could mean the organisation is unable to meet sudden increases in demand (1 development mark). Accept any other suitable response.	6
4	a		Responses could include the following: • Allows organisation to spread risk (1 mark). If one product's sales decline, another product's sales could be growing (1 development mark). • The opportunity for increased sales/profits from selling different products (1 mark) due to customers having a number of products to buy from one brand (1 development mark). • Seasonal fluctuations can be evened out (1 mark) — the company may not struggle as much if they have products that are popular at certain times of year (1 development mark). • They can meet the needs of different market segments. • Newer products at growth stage can replace those at the decline stage of the product life cycle. • Reference to analysis of Boston Matrix — resources can be allocated from poorer performing products ("dogs") to income-generating products ("stars" or "cash cows"). Accept any other suitable response.	4
	b		Responses could include the following: • Penetration pricing is used in a highly competitive market, whereas skimming pricing is used in a market with little or no competition. • Penetration pricing means that the product will be introduced at a low price, whereas skimming pricing means that the product is introduced at a high price. • With penetration pricing the price will be increased once the product has been established, whereas with skimming pricing the price is decreased as competition enters the market. • Penetration pricing is used to entice consumers to switch from other brands, whereas skimming pricing is used when the product is new or unique. • Both penetration and skimming pricing are short-term pricing strategies. • Both penetration and skimming pricing are used when introducing new products to the market. Accept any other suitable response.	3

Question			Expected Answer(s)	Max mark
4	c		Responses could include the following: • These are promotions that a manufacturer gives to the wholesaler or retailer that sells their products (definition). • Dealer loaders are one example of 'into the pipeline promotion': this involves the wholesaler/retailer receiving an extra amount free, eg five boxes for the price of four. • The manufacturer may also provide the wholesaler/retailer with staff training. • The manufacturer may provide the wholesaler/retailer with point of-sale displays. • The manufacturer could allow sale-or-return. Accept any other suitable response.	3

HIGHER FOR CfE BUSINESS MANAGEMENT
MODEL PAPER 1

SECTION 1

Question			Expected Answer(s)	Max mark
1	a		Responses could include the following:	4

			• Owned by a minimum of one shareholder.
			• Controlled by a board of directors.
			• Limited liability so owners' personal assets are not accountable if the business fails.
			• Shares are not sold on the stock market/sold privately.
			   • Control not lost to outsiders.
			   • Selling shares raises money quickly without incurring debt.
			   • Dividends paid to shareholders.
			
			Accept any other suitable response.	

	b		Responses could include the following:	3

			• The company may receive a bad reputation.
			   • Sales will decline/fewer new customers.
			   • Profits will decline leading to debt.
			• The company may close/go into administration.
			• It may be forced to seek finance from lenders and incur greater debt.
			• It may have to make staff redundant/downsize.
			• Legal disputes could arise, eg for issuing fake letters to customers.
			   • Compensation may have to be paid.
			• Fines and sanction may be imposed by regulators.
			
			Accept any other suitable response.	

	c	i	Responses could include the following:	2
			• Attempts to reduce the appeal of Wonga to children is ethical marketing which looks better for the firm's image. • Less likely to receive sanctions/fines from Ofcom. • Will receive fewer customer complaints. • Customers may trust Wonga after changing their advertising methods and therefore be more likely to borrow from them. Accept any other suitable response.	
		ii	Responses could include the following:	3
			• Monitors the communication delivered to the public. • Handles complaints regarding media and communication broadcasts. • Can request adverts or marketing to be withdrawn or changed. • Issues and regulates business licensing for TV and radio broadcasting. • Researches and reports on broadcasting activity. • Accountable to Parliament and has the power to enforce legislation. • Regulates competition within the advertising sector. Accept any other suitable response.	

Question			Expected Answer(s)	Max mark
1	d		Responses could include the following: **Gross Profit Ratio:** Gross Profit/Sales × 100 • Amount of gross profit made from every £ of sales. • Percentage of profit made (before expenses are deducted) on sales. **Net Profit Ratio:** Net Profit/Sales × 100 • Amount of net profit made from every £ of sales. • Percentage of profit made (after expenses are deducted) on sales. **Mark-up Ratio:** Gross Profit/Cost of Goods Sold × 100 • Percentage of profit to be added to cost price to find selling price. **Return on Capital Employed:** Net Profit/Capital at Start × 100 • Percentage profit earned on the capital investment. **Acid Test Ratio:** Current Assets – Stock: Current Liabilities • Ability of an organisation to pay off its short-term debts in a crisis. • Ideal 1:1. **Current Ratio:** Current Assets: Current Liabilities • Ability of an organisation to pay of its short-term debts. • Ideal 2:1. Accept any other suitable response.	6
	e		Responses could include the following: • Increases employees' skills allowing them to do a variety of tasks. • Better flexibility in the workplace. • Motivating for staff as they feel valued so less likely to resist proposed changes. • Less likely to resist management decisions. • Improved image for the company as a skilled workforce will result in better quality output. • Attract high quality staff knowing they will be trained. • Customer loyalty can occur. Accept any other suitable response.	4

	f		Responses could include the following:
			
			• **Website** using text and images online to advertise goods/services.
			  • Accessed 24/7 with a live connection.
			  • Can apply for loans through the website, increasing sales.
			  • Information can be updated quickly to better inform customers so they purchase credit.
			• **Smartphones** can be accessed on the go with wifi/3G and therefore customers can purchase credit from the comfort of their home or while travelling.
			• **Databases** can allow the company to keep records of customers' details so marketing can be targeted to specific groups increasing the chance of sales.
			• **Social Media** can be used to create viral advertising and offer promotions.
			
			Accept any other suitable response.
				3

	g		Responses could include the following: **Financial Conduct Authority** • The imposed cap on payday lending may reduce Wonga's sales. This will in turn affect profitability made on borrowing. • The pay back limitations will create a more competitive market for Wonga and its rivals, requiring an emphasis on promotion and customer service. • New regulations will require policy and products to be rewritten. **Customers** • Customers turning to loan sharks/rivals will reduce Wonga's income. • Customers can complain and therefore impact decision-making. • Refusing to pay on time results in problems for Wonga's cash flow. **Church of England** • The comments made by the Archbishop could damage Wonga's reputation. • This could lower sales from religious market segments. • Reverend Justin Welby helped small lenders compete which could put Wonga out of business if successful. • Investment could be withdrawn leaving Wonga with less funding. Accept any other suitable response.	5

SECTION 2

Question			Expected Answer(s)	Max mark

1	a		Responses could include the following:
			
			• Retained profits from previous trading periods.
			• Venture capital may provide finance when other lenders deem its use too risky.
			• Grant may be awarded if certain conditions are met.
			   • Does not need to be paid back.
			• A bank loan is paid back over time with interest.
			   • Often paid in instalments so aids budgeting.
			• Bank overdraft provides smaller amounts of finance in the short-term.
			   • Can be easily arranged over the telephone.
			   • Interest rates are often daily and are high.
			• Selling shares on the stock market can raise money quickly.
			   • A dividend needs paid if a profit is declared.
			• Hire purchasing…
			• Commercial mortgage…
			
			Accept any other suitable response.
				4

	b		Responses could include the following: • The trading account shows the gross profit/profit made from buying and selling stock over a period of time. • The profit and loss account shows the net profit/gross profit with internal expenses deducted. • Required to comply with legislation by certain types of company. • Used to inform shareholders. • Used in the valuation of a firm's worth when selling/divesting. • Can be used to apply for finance from lenders. • Required for ratio analysis/decision making. Accept any other suitable response.	3
	c		Responses could include the following: • Used to set targets which can motivate staff to work harder. • Highlight areas of surplus so that assets can be purchased. • Helps monitor the flow of cash therefore reduces the risk of overspending. • Can be delegated to departments to see which ones are underperforming. • Used to set appropriate stock levels to minimise waste. • Aids management planning, reducing the risk of poor decision-making. Accept any other suitable response.	3

2	a		Responses could include the following:
			
			• **Development stage**: profit will not be made at this stage as the product is not yet launched on the market for sale.
			• **Introduction stage**: there will be little to no profit made at this stage as the product is not well known and costs are high.
			   • However, the opposite could occur if the product is highly anticipated and much advertising has been done before its release, eg new iPhone models or top cinema releases.
			• **Growth stage**: profits should begin to rise as the sales increase.
			• **Maturity stage**: profits should be at their peak at this point.
			• **Saturation stage**: profits should be steady despite competition.
			   • The price may be lowered to compete: reducing profits.
			• **Decline stage**: profits will fall due to change in demand/fashion.
			   • A loss may be incurred before the product is withdrawn.
			
			Accept any other suitable response.
				4

Question			Expected Answer(s)	Max mark

2	b		Responses could include the following:
			
			• **Penetration pricing** is when the price is set at a low price when entering a new market.
			   • Once the product becomes popular the price is raised to be in line with competitors' prices.
			• **Destroyer pricing** involves setting a price significantly below that of competitors.
			   • Profits may be lost and this strategy cannot be sustained for any length of time.
			• **Skimming** involves using a high price initially for a new product where there is little competition.
			   • Consumers are usually willing to pay a high price for the novelty of the new product.
			   • As more competition enters the market the price is lowered.
			• **Loss leader** is when retailers advertise a range of products at unprofitable prices in order to entice customers into their stores.
			• **Competitive pricing** is when the price is set in line with competitors within an area.
			• **Promotional pricing** is when prices are reduced for a short period.
			
			Premium pricing…
			Cost-plus pricing…
			High price…
			Low price…
			
			Accept any other suitable response.
				4

	c		Responses could include the following: • Increase in outlet stores and retail parks due to the increase of cars. • More discount stores such as ALDI and LIDL are available. • Increase in online shopping and e-commerce. • Increase in home delivery. • Large stores are open for longer — some 24/7. • Increase in larger chains opening local stores. Accept any other suitable response.	2
3	a		Responses could include the following: **Quality assurance** when products are checked throughout production. **Quality control** when products are checked at the start and end of production. **Quality circles** between employees and management to discuss issues. • Communication is encouraged which is motivating. • Empowers employees to take pride in their work so fewer mistakes are made. **Quality inputs** such as an ethical and reliable supplier of raw materials. • Ensure machinery is up-to-date and well maintained. **Staff training** to improve the skills of employees. • Reduces error/less accidents. • Ensure training is on-going. • Motivated staff should ensure a quality product/service. • Benchmarking… • Quality awards eg BSI kitemark… • TQM… Accept any other suitable response.	6

	b		Responses could include the following:
			
			• Pressure to use bio-fuels and eco-friendly production processes.
			   • This may increase the cost of production.
			• Increase in regulation regarding waste management.
			   • Staff will need trained which is time consuming.
			   • Contractors for safe disposal may need employed.
			   • Licensing needs to be obtained to produce/store certain waste.
			• Penalties for high emissions and carbon costs are in effect in some countries.
			• May be difficult to obtain government support and funding/grants if the business is not complying with environmental agendas.
			• Customers are more "green" and want recyclable packaging.
			   • The business can gain a bad reputation if seen as socially irresponsible.
			
			Accept any other suitable response.
				4

Question			Expected Answer(s)	Max mark
4	a		Responses could include the following: • Internal recruitment means the employer knows the candidate's skills and qualities, unlike with external recruitment which can introduce new ideas and skills to the company. • Internal recruitment may save on induction training, whereas external recruitment will require time for the employee to adjust and learn the job. • Internal recruitment may be a quicker process because external recruitment may involve a longer advertising period or the use of other agencies. • Internal recruitment can motivate staff as it provides a promotion route, unlike external recruitment which can upset existing staff. • Internal recruitment may be cheaper as adverts can be done on the intranet/newsletter, whereas external recruitment may require adverts in national newspapers or costly ad space on job websites. • External recruitment offers a wider pool of candidates. • External recruitment is an opportunity to bring in diversity. Accept any other suitable response.	4
	b		Responses could include the following: • Relevant to the job and therefore a good investment. • Staff will feel valued and motivated if they receive training. • May become more productive. • Can lead to a greater chance of internal promotion. • May be required by law. Accept any other suitable response.	2

	c		Responses could include the following:
			
			• The line manager can set targets regarding the employee's performance.
			   • Targets can be motivating for an employee.
			   • May be linked to bonuses and rewards.
			• An opportunity for the employee to discuss problems to gain support.
			   • Reduces stress.
			• Staff can promote their achievement in an appraisal to receive positive praise.
			   • Can lead to better promotion prospects.
			• Appraisal can be linked to pay review.
			• Management can identify weak areas to arrange suitable training.
			• Areas of strength can be highlighted so management can assign relevant duties.
			
			Accept any other suitable response.
				4

HIGHER FOR CfE BUSINESS MANAGEMENT
MODEL PAPER 2

SECTION 1

Question			Expected Answer(s)	Max mark

1	a		Responses could include the following:
			
			Advantages
			• Website can be accessed 24/7 so may increase sales.
			   • Advertisement on the website will be seen by a global audience/4.3 million weekly visitors.
			   • Could sell ad space for additional income.
			• Mobile and tablet devices increased in sales by 87%.
			   • Mobile devices are convenient for shoppers as they can shop from home without having to travel to the store.
			   • 3G/wifi allow shopping from any location with a live signal.
			
			Disadvantages
			• Customers forced into re-registering with the website.
			• Many customers are not savvy with technology and find it difficult to use/site navigation problems.
			• Websites are expensive to create, upgrade and maintain.
			• Mobile technology requires a live connection/3G/wifi or it cannot connect to online shop.
			• Technical faults result in a loss of sales and profits.
			
			Accept any other suitable response.
				6

1	b		Responses could include the following: • Will be seen by many customers/4.3 million per week and can promote a good image for Elysium. • May attract high quality staff during recruitment. • Provides direction for staff which can motivate them. • Informs shareholders of the firm's aims and may encourage investment. • Used as a marketing tool to increase competitiveness between rivals. • Ethical values are stated which can give customers purchasing confidence. Accept any other suitable response.	2
1	c		Responses could include the following: • Roland Martin (Chief Executive) can make poor decisions in his favour over the firm's interest which can be costly and incur high risk. • Shareholders can vote at the AGM to appoint key directors/influence decision-making. • Shareholders can sell their shares which may lower the value of the firm. • Customers can shop at rival stores lowering Elysium's income. • Could complain resulting in more refunds/returns. • Retail/equity analysts can negatively report on performance which can impact the reputation of the company. Accept any other suitable response.	4
1	d	i	Responses could include the following: *Advantages* • May receive government grants/incentives to locate abroad. • Risk is reduced as the company will become larger. • Increase in sales and profits from new markets. • May be able to exploit economies of scale. • Reduced labour costs overseas. *Disadvantages* • Social differences may require different stock/promotion decisions. • Different legislation may limit decision-making. • Different taxation rules may require expensive accounting processes. • Language barriers make it difficult to communicate effectively. Accept any other suitable response.	5

Question			Expected Answer(s)	Max mark

1	d	ii	Responses could include the following:
			
			• **Selling shares** to raise money quickly.
			   • A dividend is paid if a profit is made.
			   • A loss of ownership can occur as many shares may be sold affecting decision making in the long term.
			• **Bank loan** is where money is borrowed over a period of time and paid back with interest.
			   • Interest rates can be high.
			   • Do not need to pay back cash all at once.
			   • Instalments help with cash flow and budgeting.
			• **Retained profits** is surplus cash held back from previous trading periods.
			   • No interest or repayment involved.
			• **Overdraft** allows a company to withdraw funds to an agreed amount.
			   • May have higher daily interest/penalty for unplanned withdrawals.
			   • Simple to arrange, ie over the phone.
			   • Provides fast access to overdraft funds.
			• Commercial mortgage…
			• Grants…
			• Venture capital…
			Accept any other suitable response.
				4

1	e		Responses could include the following: • Quick method of growth because a franchisee enters into an agreement to setup a new outlet. • Can grow with little investment as the franchisee will often pay a down payment. • Provides a source of income as the franchisee will pay a royalty. • Ideas can be shared between the franchise owners, making the firm more competitive. • Risk is shared between the franchiser and the franchisee. Accept any other suitable response.	3

1	f		Responses could include the following:
			
			• Ensures there is a fair and equal policy within the workplace to prevent discrimination.
			   • Have sanctions for internal bullying, harassment and victimisation.
			• Uses an objective selection process such as a panel interview with an external interviewer to reduce any bias.
			• Upholds complaints made and investigates any discrimination at work with regard to the nine protected characteristics.
			• All staff trained in current employment legislation.
			• Ensures contracts are issued within the time legally specified.
			• Equal payment practices.
			• Ensures the workplace, working conditions and expectations are fair for all.
			   • Budget for ramps and railing etc for disability/accessibility.
			
			Accept any other suitable response.
				4

1	g		Responses could include the following: Strategic and Tactical • Strategic decisions affect the whole of Elysium's operations, whereas tactical decisions are about how to achieve Elysium's aims. • Strategic decisions are made by the Chief Executive/board of directors, whereas a tactical decision is made by middle-level management. • Strategic decisions are normally made over a long period of time, whereas tactical decisions are made on a medium-term basis. Operational and… • Operational decisions are short-term decisions… • Operational decisions are made by all staff/low-level staff… • Operational decisions are day-to-day decisions… Accept any other suitable response.	2

SECTION 2

Question			Expected Answer(s)	Max mark
1	a		Responses could include the following: • Stocking Fair Trade goods is seen as ethical, improving the firm's image. • Customers may be willing to pay more so a higher price can be charged. • Increases profitability/sales. • Customers may be loyal to Fair Trade goods as sales support farmers. • Improves social responsibility — farmers will be better paid. Accept any other suitable response.	2
	b		Responses could include the following: • Job production is labour-intensive, whereas batch production may use more capital-intensive processes. • Job production allows for unique products to be made, whereas with batch production the entire batch must be changed. • Job production may be expensive as only one product/service can be done at a time, unlike with batch production which can exploit economies of scale. • Job production may be more motivating due to the variety of the tasks, unlike batch production which may be repetitive. • Job production may be able to charge a higher price. • Batch production produces more/better productivity. • Batch production means an entire batch is wasted if errors are made. Accept any other suitable response.	4
	c		Responses could include the following: • Workers and managers meet to discuss improvements in production/service. • Allows for idea generation from the workers who do the job. • Can improve the quality of work/better output. • Workers may see this as a chore and resist/become stressed. • Workers can feel valued by participating in decision-making. • Less likely to resist changes. • Production time may be lost while a quality circle is taking place. Accept any other suitable response.	4
2	a		Responses could include the following: • A business may be forced to sell its assets. • More susceptible to a takeover/buyout from its competitors. • Finance may be needed, incurring debt. • Lenders may be less likely to offer finance/funding. • Suppliers may be less likely to offer trade credit. • Customers may not purchase from the company lowering its sales. • Poor reputation means fewer quality candidates apply for posts. • Employees may be made redundant. Accept any other suitable response.	3
	b		Responses could include the following: • Offer discounts to encourage prompt payment from debtors. • Offer discounts/promote cash sales to increase sales. • Sell any unused assets. • Reduce loans by, eg increasing number of investors. • Apply for debt factoring. • Hire purchase/lease assets. • Extended credit, ie on an overdraft/loan. • Purchase less from suppliers. • Introduce JIT. • Cut internal expenses, eg staff redundancy. Accept any other suitable response.	4

Question			Expected Answer(s)	Max mark
	c		Responses could include the following: • Automatically calculates figures in budgets using formulae. • Minimises the chance of arithmetical error. • Formulae are dynamic and so update automatically, saving time. • Charts can be created to compare finances between products. • Spreadsheet templates can be setup saving time. • Can be easily amended/edited. • Can be securely stored with a password. Accept any other suitable response.	3

3	a		Responses could include the following:
			
			• National newspapers can reach a large/regional audience.
			  • Adverts are only in black and white/grayscale.
			  • Decreasing effectiveness due to the increase of online news.
			• Job centres allow for specialist staff to advertise/recruit.
			• Specialist websites can target the required type of candidates.
			  • Can be an expensive method of advertising.
			• Apps on smartphones/tablets send notification of new posts to candidates who subscribe.
			  • Applications can be done online.
			• Advertisement on the radio can be heard by commuters.
			  • Can pay to play at core times, ie between 7 and 9 am.
			
			Accept any other suitable response.
				4

	b		Responses could include the following:
			
			• **Autocratic leadership** may lower motivation as staff feel they have no say.
			  • However, some staff may respond well to regimented instruction.
			• **Participative leadership** means staff may feel valued because they are involved.
			• **Laissez-Faire leadership** may empower staff as they are given freedom over a task.
			  • Some staff may feel there is no clear direction and lose motivation.
			
			Accept any other suitable response.
				3

	c		Responses could include the following: • **Advice:** offers advice on matters such as contracts of employment, human resource policies and legislation. • **Conciliation:** will intervene, if requested, in a dispute and offer a solution that both parties will accept. • **Arbitration:** assesses the problem and recommends a course of action which both parties agree to abide by. Accept any other suitable response.	3
4	a		Responses could include the following: • Allows an organisation to anticipate changes in consumer taste. • Keeps the organisation ahead of its competitors. • Ensures product meets the needs of consumers. • Helps identify a gap in the market. • Produce new products/improve existing ones. • Finding a unique product can become very profitable. • Provides information about the best place to sell the product. • Gives information about the price consumers are willing to pay. • Helps identify the best way to promote a product. • Reduces risk of failure when launching a new product. • Products/business promoted at the same time. Accept any other suitable response.	2
	b		Responses could include the following: • Changing the price, such as lowering it, will attract customers on a lower income to purchase it. • Improving the product by creating new features will increase sales. • Changing the advertising method means the product will be seen by different people. • Change the use for the product which will target a different market segment. • Change the packaging therefore making the product more appealing. • Change the name/rebrand the product as this will attract new customers. • Change the place of sale, eg online which could result in global sales. Accept any other suitable response.	4

Question			Expected Answer(s)	Max mark

4	c		Responses could include the following:
			
			• Purchases goods from the manufacturer and adds a mark-up to create a profit.
			  • May purchase in bulk and break items down to sell to retailers.
			• Can distribute goods to retailers on behalf of the manufacturer.
			  • Saves travel time and fuel costs for the manufacturer.
			• The wholesaler carries the risk of fashion changes.
			  • Manufacturer does not have cash tied up in stock if sold to the wholesaler.
			• May label and package goods for the manufacturer.
			• Large orders will be placed as the wholesaler will buy in bulk from the manufacturer.
			• Reduced warehousing and storage required by the manufacturer if stock is sold to the wholesaler quickly.
			
			Accept any other suitable response.
				4

HIGHER FOR CfE BUSINESS MANAGEMENT
MODEL PAPER 3

SECTION 1

Question			Expected Answer(s)	Max mark
1	a		Responses could include the following: • Mary's Meals aims to support a school feeding programme for children all over the world, whereas a public sector organisation aims to provide a service to a local/regional area. • Mary's Meals has an objective to maximise donations, whereas a public sector organisation has the objective to use public funds effectively. • Both Mary's Meals and a public sector organisation aim to provide the best service possible. • Both organisations aim to support education in the community. • Both organisations have the objective to be socially responsible. • Both organisations aim to support people in poverty. Accept any other suitable response.	3

	b		Responses could include the following:
			
			• It may be cheaper to import food/materials but this would create more pollution which could result in a poor image for the company.
			  • Importing goods would not support local business which could lower respect in the area.
			• Legislation differences may exist limiting the activities of Mary's Meals.
			  • It can be expensive to train staff in new legislation requirements.
			  • Quotas could be imposed limiting business activity.
			• Varied taxation and accounting requirements may be imposed between countries which could complicate financial transactions.
			• Cultural differences could result in the need to retrain staff or risk offending locals.
			• Working hours and conditions may vary which could result in HR issues for transferred staff.
			• Language barriers can exist making communication problematic.
			
			Accept any other suitable response.
				5

	c		Responses could include the following:
			
			• **Website** using text and images online to market to a global audience.
			  • Accessed 24/7 from any location with a live connection.
			  • Can donate through the website increasing income.
			  • Information can be updated quickly to better inform stakeholders.
			• **Celebrity endorsement** such as Gerard Butler can raise awareness amongst fans.
			• **Animation** such as the Saving Grace story showing moving images and sound to convey information.
			• **Sponsorship** of a school will raise awareness at events in return for support.
			• **Stage work** such as film-making to raise awareness to a large audience.
			
			Accept any other suitable response.
				5

	d		Responses could include the following: • Creates a positive image for the organisation which can allow them to attract high quality staff in the recruitment process. • May allow them to receive grants and incentives by complying with government policy. • More likely to receive donations and therefore increase funds. • A good reputation from good word of mouth will raise awareness of the organisation. • Help to achieve the company mission statement and objectives. Accept any other suitable response.	3

Question			Expected Answer(s)	Max mark

1	e		Responses could include the following:
			
			• **Postal surveys** can be sent out to donors' homes and returned.
			  • Target an area at a relatively low cost.
			  • Low success rate as many people consider postal surveys as junk mail .
			• **Face-to-face interviews** provide instant feedback/clarification.
			  • Allows for body language/facial expressions to be seen which can improve communication.
			  • Can persuade people to donate more effectively if face-to-face.
			  • Poor interviewer/personality may intimidate.
			• **Customer/employee focus groups** give a range of opinions from a diverse group.
			  • May be expensive to run as often members need paid.
			• **Telephone surveys** often carried out by calling and asking questions remotely.
			  • Often seen as a nuisance and therefore may suffer for a low response rate.
			• Online survey…
			• Desk research…
			
			Accept any other suitable response.
				6

	f	i	Responses could include the following: • Due to an increase in promotional methods used by Mary's Meals. • A change of culture as society becomes more responsive to ethical businesses. • More disposable income in the economy. • An increase in fundraising and charitable events. • The website allows for donations to be made online. Accept any other suitable response.	2
		ii	Responses could include the following: • Donations do not have to be paid back unlike a bank loan which requires the amount to be repaid over time with interest. • Donations vary in amount unlike a bank loan which is a specified amount. • A bank loan can be requested up front at a far greater amount than donations for expansion purposes. • Donations may take longer to receive, whereas a bank loan could be delivered in full if terms are met. • Commercial mortgage is taken out against a property, whereas a bank overdraft is short-term access to finance which is expected to be paid off quickly. • Venture capital… • Government grant… • Hire purchase/leasing… Accept any other suitable response.	2
	g		Responses could include the following: • An absence of volunteers/available staff could result in low productivity and fewer children being fed. • A lack of donations/funding or appropriate budgeting can result in reduced services. • Some volunteers/employees may lack skill which could lead to poor workmanship. • Managers may lack experience to launch projects successfully which can damage the organisation's reputation. • There may be a lack of information available leading to poor decision-making. • Poorly maintained technology could break down resulting in a halt in service. • Networks and company wifi availability allows its volunteers to stay better informed around the world. Accept any other suitable response.	4

SECTION 2

Question			Expected Answer(s)	Max mark

1	a		Responses could include the following:
			
			• Increases employees' skills allowing them to do a variety of tasks.
			  • Better flexibility in the workplace.
			• Fewer accidents/less waste as staff are skilled.
			• Motivating for staff as they feel valued.
			  • Can lead to an increase in productivity.
			• Skilled workforce will result in better quality output.
			  • Improved image for the company.
			• Attract high quality staff knowing they will be trained.
			• Customer loyalty can occur.
			
			Accept any other suitable response.
				5

	b		Responses could include the following: • Autocratic leadership is where the leader has complete control/authority, whereas laissez-faire empowers individuals to complete a task within a set time with little involvement. • Autocratic leadership can risk micromanagement, whereas laissez-faire can empower staff. • Autocratic leadership works well when time is limited or staff are uncertain, whereas laissez-faire works well in creative industries. • Both can result in limited communication. • Both can lead to staff stress levels being high. Accept any other suitable response.	3
	c		Responses could include the following: • Allows for management to review an employee's performance to determine suitable payment. • Provides a dialogue for employees to present their achievements to negotiate payment. • 360° appraisal/peer appraisal can result in many opinions from different colleagues/departments so an objective payment decision made. Accept any other suitable response.	2
2	a		Responses could include the following: Profitability • Used to evaluate an organisation's purchasing policy. • Can help set an appropriate selling price. • May be used to negotiate the cost of stock/supplier discounts. • Allows for expenses to be reviewed to avoid overspending. Liquidity • Measures the ability of a firm to repay debt. • May be used by lenders/creditors to determine repayment periods. • Can review asset purchases/hire purchases/leasing decisions. • Used to evaluate debts and credit limits. Efficiency • Measures how successfully a business has used the capital invested. Accept any other suitable response.	6

	b		Responses could include the following:
			
			• Shows movements of cash so helps forecast sales/production.
			• Used to set targets to increase productivity.
			  • Staff may become motivated.
			• Allows for the comparing of actual and estimated results.
			  • Can be used to evaluate for better planning in the future.
			• Highlights areas of strength to adjust spending decisions.
			• Shows projected areas of deficit to allow for finance to be arranged.
			
			Accept any other suitable response.
				4

3	a		Responses could include the following: • Purchase only what is required. • Recycle more throughout production. • Quality assure to identify mistakes early. • Train staff so fewer mistakes are made. • Use ethical suppliers. Accept any other suitable response.	3

Question			Expected Answer(s)	Max mark

3	b		Responses could include the following:
			
			• Cash not tied-up in stock and therefore can be used elsewhere.
			• Less space is needed saving on storage/rent costs.
			   • Insurance may be reduced.
			   • Security and labour costs are reduced.
			• Reduction in theft as it is easier to control a limited supply of stock.
			• Reduction in waste.
			
			Accept any other suitable response.
				3

	c		Responses could include the following: *Advantages* • More environmentally friendly than road/air. • Ideal for heavy products/large quantities. • Less traffic implications than road. • Less likely to be limited by weather unlike air. *Disadvantages* • Requires a rail network which is not suitable in some rural areas. • Cannot offer door-to-door service. • Often requires the support of road to make a complete delivery. • Requires specialist freight terminals to load products. • Limited globally, unlike sea and air. Accept any other suitable response.	4
4	a		Responses could include the following: • More promotion opportunities. • Narrow span of control may mean more support/supervision. • Clearer structure makes it easier to navigate to relevant staff. • Ideal for large firms as minimises the conflict of responsibility. Accept any other suitable response.	3
	b		Responses could include the following: • Employees' pay may not reflect their work demands or performance. • The working environment/conditions may be poor with no finance being invested. • Financial benefits and rewards may not be given. • Overtime may become an expectation. • Employees may feel pressured and stressed to meet demands. • Staff may not be employed despite a requirement for more labour. • Staff may not receive expensive training. • Promotion routes may be limited. Accept any other suitable response.	3

	c		Responses could include the following:
			
			• Improved customer satisfaction from a positive experience with staff.
			   • Customer loyalty can occur leading to repeat custom.
			• Consistent culture across all departments/branches making it easier to train staff/standardise processes.
			• Increased staff motivation as they associate with the aims of the firm.
			   • Reduced absenteeism/lower staff turnover.
			• Transfers between departments/branches is easier.
			• More opportunities can entice high quality staff to apply.
			
			Accept any other suitable response.
				4

HIGHER FOR CfE BUSINESS MANAGEMENT
MODEL PAPER 4

SECTION 1

Question			Expected Answer(s)	Max mark
1	a		Responses could include the following: • Greater flexibility as they can arrange training to suit the work schedule. • Training can be better tailored to the needs of the staff. • More regular training may be arranged due to better availability. • Specialist staff will be employed to provide high quality training. • Reduced costs from when they were using external agencies. • Staff may feel motivated if they receive specialist training. • Specialist training will increase the chance of promotion within Arnold Clark. • Additional income can be earned by training other firms. • Strong working relationship can be built from training other firms. • Increases Arnold Clark's competitiveness in the marketplace. • May attract high quality staff if they know Arnold Clark invests in training. Accept any other suitable response.	4

	b		Responses could include the following:
			
			Diversification
			• Arnold Clark set up firms in different markets, eg insurance.
			  • Provides different income streams from the core business activity.
			  • Reduces risk as businesses are in unrelated markets.
			
			Acquisitions/Take-over
			• Arnold Clark purchased other dealerships.
			  • Used to quickly expand as staff and assets of a firm are purchased when acquired.
			  • Can be used to eliminate Arnold Clark's competition.
			  • Can absorb the firm's clients and sales.
			
			Organic Growth
			• Arnold Clark grew from internal sources/funding/retained profits.
			  • Opened up many new branches.
			  • Setup other areas of business, eg insurance services/offered new services.
			  • Bid for contracts to earn additional income to expand.
			  • Employed more staff.
			  • Purchased more cars in stock to offer more variety for sale.
			
			Accept any other suitable response.
				6

	c	i	Responses could include the following: • Product grouping is when staff are organised around a specific service/product and will have different areas of expertise. • Each group has responsibility/autonomy in their area. • Can lead to internal competition. • Group may lose track of the organisation's goals and only be concerned with their area only. • Easy to identify areas of the company that are doing well. • More responsive to change. • Duplication of resources may occur. Accept any other suitable response.	2

Question			Expected Answer(s)	Max mark
1	c	ii	Responses could include the following: Autocratic is where the leader takes full control • Less involvement from staff in decision-making. • Lack of trust present. • Employees' stress may be increased. • May be demotivating for staff. Democratic is where the leader allows workers to contribute in decision-making • Upward communication encouraged. • Delegating and empowerment better used. • Can result in better motivation by staff as they feel valued. • Decision-making may be time consuming. • Staff may encounter conflict due to disagreement. Laissez Faire is where the leader empowers individuals to complete a task within a set time with little involvement • Staff may feel stressed with increased responsibility. • The freedom offered can increase job satisfaction. • Employees feel trusted and respected. • Leader takes on a role of guidance/facilitator. Accept any other suitable response.	2
	d		Responses could include the following: *Advantages* • Helps meet the criteria of government agendas and therefore could qualify for grants/incentives/tax relief. • Arnold Clark's company image will be enhanced making them more competitive. • Higher sales/customer loyalty. • Ethical practice attracts high quality staff in the recruitment process. • More likely to retain staff who believe in the firm's policy. • Less likely to receive complaints/protests if the company acts responsibly. *Disadvantages* • It can be costly to setup and maintain responsible business practice. • May require Arnold Clark to disregard some opportunities that may not be seen as ethical/opportunity cost. • Staff may require extensive training which is time consuming. Accept any other suitable response.	4

	e		Responses could include the following:
			
			• GTG training will mean staff are skilled and capable of their job.
			   • Less likely to make mistakes/reduce waste.
			   • Well-trained staff promote a good image to customers.
			   • Better relationships with customers mean they will return.
			• Stocking a huge choice of cars give customers variety and choice improving their experience.
			   • Increasing the chance of a sale.
			• Offering a good trade-in value and price on new cars makes Arnold Clark competitive in comparison to rivals.
			• Promoting an excellent service statistically at 97% means customers will spread good word of mouth.
			• Additional services such as ACCIST and a free accident management service give customers good value for money.
			• Quality control measures, such as 120-point inspection before being sold, mean fewer complaints/returns are unlikely.
			• Competitive pricing.
			• After-care services.
			
			Accept any other suitable response.
				5

Question			Expected Answer(s)	Max mark
	f		Responses could include the following: • Customers can browse the website at any time meaning they have access to the latest price changes and offers. • The website allows customers to search car models/browse stock saving them the hassle of travelling to the store. • The website can be used to book a test drive or speak to a consultant online which improves the customer experience. • The website can be used to compare prices with rivals showing Arnold Clark as a competitive firm and possibly leading to more sales. Accept any other suitable response.	2
	g		Responses could include the following: Competition from other garages • Competitors may lower their price forcing Arnold Clark to do the same. • Lower prices may mean less profitability. • Competitors may launch promotional materials/advertisements forcing Arnold Clark to invest in further costly marketing. A downturn in the economy • People will have less disposable income and therefore sales may drop. • Suppliers may be less likely to offer trade credit/discounts. • Lenders may be less likely to offer longer repayment periods or loan on risky ventures. • High unemployment may make it easier to recruit labour workers. An increase in the price of fuel • Will increase the internal expenses at Arnold Clark. • More people will use public transport/walk/cycle and fewer car sales may be made. • May increase the sale of hybrid cars. Accept any other suitable response.	5

SECTION 2

Question			Expected Answer(s)	Max mark

1	a		Responses could include the following:
			
			• **Spreadsheet** software can be used to automatically calculate figures in budgets using formulae.
			  • Minimises the chance of arithmetical error.
			  • Formulae are dynamic so update automatically saving time.
			  • Charts can be created to compare finances between products.
			• **Word Processing** software can be used to write letters to the bank regarding finances.
			  • Used to create templates for invoicing etc.
			• **Presentation** software can be used to convey financial performance to stakeholders at a meeting.
			• **Database** software can be used to store financial records or customer accounts.
			• **Online banking** can be used to make payments quickly between accounts.
			
			Accept any other suitable response.
				4

	b		Responses could include the following: Profitability • Increase in income, eg set a higher selling price. • Offer promotions/advertise. • Source a cheaper supplier. • Negotiate cheaper supplier deals/discounts. • Set appropriate stock levels. • Increase supervision on stock to deter theft. • Minimise wastage. • Set targets to motivate staff to work harder. • Limit overtime to reduce costs. Liquidity • Improve credit control by chasing up cash from debtors. • Budget more effectively to ensure cash is available. • Pay creditors on time or early to receive a discount. • Avoid high interest rates on borrowed finance. • Limit the amount purchased on credit/in an overdraft. Accept any other suitable response.	6

Question			Expected Answer(s)	Max mark
2	a		Responses could include the following: • Reduced risk because of the alternative income from other products. • Better cash flow and possibly profitability. • Same resources can be used to produce varied goods therefore avoiding duplication of resources/staff/machinery. • Easier to launch new products if they are all branded increasing the chance of success/sales. • It may be more competitive to have a varied portfolio as the firm can share experience across different product groupings. • Improved image as loyal customers feel they have choice across the brand. Accept any other suitable response.	4
	b		Responses could include the following: • Reduce the price to attract lower income customers. • Change the packaging to create new appeal. • Change the product use to attract to a different market. • Introduce a new variety or flavour. • Rebrand/rename the product. • Put on a special offer/promotion. • Change the place of sale, eg online. • Change the advertising method. Accept any other suitable response.	4
	c		Responses could include the following: • Lowering the price of a product may increase sales from customers with less disposable income. • Once they have tried the product they may become loyal and continue purchasing once the price increases. • Destroyer pricing will lower the price of the product in comparison to rivals making it the more competitive option for purchase. • Significantly lowering the price can portray the product as inferior and some customers may no longer purchase it. • A loss may be made on the product using this strategy resulting in lower profitability. Accept any other suitable response.	2
3	a		Responses could include the following: • Centralised inventory may reduce the chance of theft as stock is easier to monitor, whereas decentralised stock can result in a loss of control. • Centralised warehousing may make it easier to transport goods from one accessible location, whereas decentralised warehousing can increase the number of trips required resulting in high fuel costs. • Centralised warehousing reduces the duplication of resources, saving money, whereas decentralised warehousing may require multiple security measures/administrators to be in place. • Centralised inventory increases the risk of all stock being damaged by fire/flood etc. unlike decentralised which separates stock to remote locations. • Decentralised stock may be closer to the market, reducing transport costs and time, whereas centralised stock may require longer delivery/lead times to individual locations. Accept any other suitable response.	3

	b		Responses could include the following:
			
			• Automated machinery can work in hazardous/dangerous conditions.
			• Can manufacture with precision on delicate technology chips.
			• Can create large volumes 24/7 — no requirement for breaks.
			  • Reduced labour costs.
			• Deliver consistent quality of goods.
			  • Less likely to see returns.
			  • Reduces waste.
			• Massively speeds up production which satisfies large demands/orders.
			• Technical faults may occur halting production.
			• Staff may be made redundant, lowering motivation/morale.
			• High initial costs for purchasing machinery/training staff.
			
			Accept any other suitable response.
				5

Question			Expected Answer(s)	Max mark
	c		Responses could include the following: • Undercover researcher can give an accurate account of a customer's experience. • A mystery shopper can identify areas of strength to praise staff. • A mystery shopper can discover areas of weakness to identify training needs. • Obtains up-to-date/primary information for decision-making. • Can be used to research rival firms. Accept any other suitable response.	2
4	a		Responses could include the following: • Work-based qualifications are relevant to the job and therefore improve performance. • Staff feel motivated if the organisation supports their training needs and therefore may be more productive. • Reduced absenteeism/lowers staff turnover. • Staff may have better promotion prospects if they improve their skillset and therefore become more empowered. Accept any other suitable response.	3

	b		Responses could include the following:
			
			• **IQ testing** assesses a candidate's mental ability.
			   • Often focuses on literacy, numeracy and problem-solving skills.
			• **Attainment testing** determines a candidate's knowledge and skills.
			   • May be practical in nature such as a touch-typing test.
			• **Psychometric testing** assesses a candidate's behaviour and traits.
			   • Candidates may be given moral and ethical scenarios.
			• **Medical testing** assesses the candidate's fitness for the job.
			• **Aptitude testing** assesses natural ability/potential.
			
			Accept any other suitable response.
				4

	c		Responses could include the following: • Represents the rights of workers within an organisation or industry. • Bargains on behalf of workers for fair/good working conditions. • Deals with health and safety requirements for workers. • Negotiates fair payment. • Coordinates industrial action if necessary. • Handles matters relating to equality/harassment/victimisation. • Offers advice and legal support. Accept any other suitable response.	3

HIGHER FOR CfE BUSINESS MANAGEMENT 2015

SECTION 1

Question			Expected Answer(s)	Max mark
1	a	i	• The type of production used to produce Google's headquarters is Job Production which is producing a single product/one off product/products to exact requirements	1
		ii	**Advantages** • The headquarters can be designed to exact specifications • A higher price can be charged • It allows the customer to change the design/make alterations during the process • More motivated staff • Will improve an organisation's competitiveness if it is the only one that can provide non-standard products **Disadvantages** • The wages paid will need to be higher to reflect staff skills • This will increase the overall final price of the product which may put some customers off • There can be higher than average R&D costs • Costs are high as a variety of machinery/tools are required which may often be laying idle • Lead times can be lengthy	5
	b		• Allows organisation to spread risk over different markets • Can meet the needs of different market segments • 'Cash cows' can fund other, riskier, ventures • 'Stars' can allow a business to be a market leader • 'Problem Child' products give businesses opportunity to invest • 'Dogs' should be divested • Increased profits can arise from selling different products • Newer products can replace those at the end of the life cycle • A range of products increases brand awareness • Easier to launch new products with large existing portfolio	5

	c		• Google uses flexible working patterns which means staff work when is best suited to them/ when they are most productive
			• Staff can work from home/where they want which might motivate them to be more productive
			• Open plan/relaxed office layout encourages collaboration which means better communication and idea sharing
			   • This will also lead to better decisions being made
			• Perks such as pool tables, bowling alleys, gyms etc will mean staff are motivated and will work to a better standard
			   • This will also mean staff turnover will also be low meaning quality trained staff aren't lost to competition
			   • Perks will also attract the best staff to Google meaning they have an advantage over the competition
			• Roof gardens, coffee shops etc will encourage staff to communicate with each other in a relaxed informal way, leading to better decision making
			• Casual dress code will mean there is a relaxed environment in which to work in/will mean staff want to come to the office
			• Strong corporate identity through corporate colours/language and jargon etc which will mean employees feel part of the organisation
			• Use of relaxed and informal language means staff feel comfortable working there and perform well
				4

	d	i	• Revenue (sales): The amount of money received for selling goods or services during the year • Gross Profit: The profit made from buying and selling OR • GP is calculated by deducting cost of sales from sales revenue	2
		ii	Possible trends include: • Profit has increased • Gross profit has increased • Profit for the year (Net Profit) has increased	1

Question	Expected Answer(s)	Max mark
e	**Horizontal integration** • Google could acquire (takeover) or merge with a business in the same sector of industry as it **Vertical integration** • Google could acquire (takeover) or merge with a business in an earlier (backward) or • Later (forward) sector of industry as it **Conglomerate integration/diversification** • Google could acquire (takeover) or merge with a business in a completely different market as it **Outsourcing** • Google could contract out some of its procedures (eg catering, admin etc) • To allow it to concentrate on core activities **Divestment** • Google could sell off parts of its business to raise money to fund external growth eg takeover Management buy-in... Merger... Takeover... Asset stripping...	4
f	**Advantages** • Fresh, new ideas/skills are brought into the business • Wider pool of talent to choose from • There is no 'gap' created by promoting from within • It can avoid jealousy being created from one existing staff member being promoted over another **Disadvantages** • Timely to recruit and select from such a vast pool • Induction training will have to be carried out • Production time lost • Can be costly • Staff may be de-motivated because there is no internal promotion • New employee is unknown to the organisation	5
g	• Google has a charitable arm called Google.org which promotes renewable energy • Funding environmental research proves Google is willing to pay to help the environment • Google uses solar panels at the Googleplex to reduce its carbon footprint • Google focuses on air quality/letting less harmful chemicals into the environment • Google offers free EV charging stations for employees vehicles to reduce emissions • Google treats its staff well eg • Publicity in Fortune: Best Company To Work For • Perks such as flexible working, gym equipment etc	3

SECTION 2

Question			Expected Answer(s)	Max mark
2	a		• Free samples to try • Free entry to competitions • Demonstrations of products - let customers see/try new product before buying • Credit facilities allow customers to buy and pay back over a period of time • Free gift with purchase of the new product • BOGOF – buy new product, get another item free • Free delivery with purchase • Offering discounts/promotional pricing	4
	b		• Type of Product – suitable transportation/storage for type of product; product durability eg electrical, frozen food, flowers, liquid, livestock • Finance available – if finance is limited this may affect the choice of channel selected • Image of Product – channel should reflect the quality of the product eg high quality distributed through exclusive, up-market retailers • Legal restrictions – some products can only be sold in certain ways/places eg cigarettes/alcohol/medicines • Where the product is in its life cycle – as it progresses through growth to maturity it needs to be more available to the market • Distribution capability of the organisation – does it have transport or does this need to be outsourced • Technical products – if highly technical it may need to be demonstrated through direct sales	4

Question			Expected Answer(s)	Max mark
	c		• Random sampling is when respondents are picked randomly **whereas** quota is picked from a group of people with specific characteristics • Random uses pre-selected respondents who must be interviewed **whereas** Quota allows researcher to find respondents who fit the characteristics required • Random is expensive to carry out because specific respondents must be interviewed and contacted until they are available **whereas** Quota is less expensive as the interviewer simply needs to find suitable respondents • Random sampling reduces biased results because of method of selection of respondents but bias can occur with quota sampling as the interviewer decides who to question Accept any other suitable response.	2
3	a		**Advantages** • Stock may be ordered in bulk and economies of scale taken advantage of • Reduced risk of pilferage as staff may be employed to monitor issues of stock • Stock is maintained in appropriate conditions which reduces waste • No space is taken up in departments with storage • Specialist staff handle stock more efficiently • Centralised warehouse can be cheaper than using multiple warehouses • Centralised ensures consistent stock handling procedures **Disadvantages** • More time is taken to access stock – physically moving the stock to department and the paperwork involved • Additional staff increases costs • Cost of specialist equipment and storage facilities • Not reflective of actual stock usage in each division/branch	4

	b		• It is harder to cope with unexpected changes in demand which means customers may go elsewhere
			• If customers are forced to go elsewhere for a product they may be lost completely to a competitor
			• Could cause delays in production or possibly halt production as there are no raw materials to use in production
			  • Which can mean paying for workers who aren't producing any goods
			• Continually ordering stock can mean increased administration costs
			• Increased transport costs due to the number of deliveries taking place
			  • Can also increase carbon footprint
			• Increased unit costs due to making small orders as opposed to buying in bulk
			• Relies on good communication/relationships with suppliers to work effectively
				4

	c		• Fairtrade certification improves the image of the organisation • Attracts consumers who have positive attitudes towards products which are ethically made • The Fairtrade trademark can be used as a marketing tool • The trademark shows international standards have been met • Higher prices can be charged for Fairtrade products • May attract staff who wish to work for an ethical company	2
4	a		• They help to highlight periods when cash flow problems may occur; • This allows the organisation to take corrective action • Cash budgets can be used to secure borrowing/show potential investors • They can be used to make comparisons between actual spending and targeted spending • They can show periods of surplus cash which could be used for capital investment • They can be used to give departments/managers a budget/target to focus on • They can be used to aid future financial planning • They can help to measure performance of organisation/departments Accept any other suitable response.	4
	b		• To measure the organisation's market share • To compare costs eg expenses • To compare GP%/NP% • To find out if they may be a target for takeover • To help their own decision making • To compare prices • To offer better salaries Accept any other suitable response.	2

Question			Expected Answer(s)	Max mark
	c		**Share issue** • Shareholders become owners of plc which may mean founders lose control • Large sums of money can be raised by this method **Government grant** • May take a long time to secure the grant • Must meet specific conditions to secure grant • Does not have to be paid back **Bank loan** • Simple and fast way to increase finance in business • Interest charges may affect cash flow in a negative way • Repaid in instalments which aids budgeting **Commercial mortgage** • Repaid with interest over long term **Debentures** • Interest is charged and may affect cash flow **Venture capital/business angels** • Will provide capital when banks think it is too risky; advise and support may also be provided to help improve/grow the business **Hire purchase…** **Leasing…**	4

5	a		• Maslow's theory classifies human needs and how they are related to each other (hierarchy)
			• A person starts at the bottom of the hierarchy and will initially seek to satisfy basic needs eg food and shelter
			  • These can be satisfied through pay
			• Once these needs have been satisfied they are no longer a motivator
			• The next level which is security and protection (safety needs)
			  • Job security/safe working environment
			• The next level is social/love and belonging needs where most people want to belong to a group
			  • Working with colleagues who provide support, teamwork communication
			• Esteem needs are about being given recognition for a job well done
			  • A promotion might achieve this
			• Self-actualisation is how people realise their potential
			  • May be measured by the extent of success and/or challenge at work
			• If management can identify which level each employee has reached they can decide on suitable rewards
				4

	b		• Employees will have their chance to discuss changes or grievances so will feel happier and more secure in the workplace • It will be easier to introduce change within the organisation as staff will become flexible with suggestions from management • Disputes are less likely to arise as the workers will have been consulted and understand what it is that the employer is trying to achieve through the changes and why the changes are necessary • Good employee relations mean that the workforce will be committed and will help ensure the business meets its objectives • The organisation will gain a good image for treating its employees correctly and maintaining good employee relations and therefore will attract new employees easily	3

	c		• Avoids discrimination within the workplace
			• Requires organisations to promote equality
			• They must ensure that their recruitment policies are compliant with the act
			• They must have comprehensive anti-discrimination and harassment policies in place
			• Action needs to be taken against barriers that prevent employees with protected characteristics from carrying out their job, making it accessible for them
			  • Ensuring disability access in the workplace may be costly
			• The organisation must investigate any accusations of discrimination and take action where necessary
			• The organisation may face legal action
			  • Could result in fines/sanctions
			  • Reputation may be negatively affected
				3

[END OF MARKING INSTRUCTIONS]

Acknowledgements

Permission has been sought from all relevant copyright holders and Hodder Gibson is grateful for the use of the following:

Information has been adapted from pages 4—25 of J Sainsbury plc Annual Report and Financial Statements 2013. Reproduced by kind permission of J Sainsbury plc (SQP pages 2 to 5);
Sainsbury's market share — 'Kantar Worldpanel total till roll for the 52 weeks to 17 March 2013,' is reproduced by kind permission of Kantar Worldpanel (SQP page 4);
An image © Wonga.com (Model Paper 1 page 2);
Extract from the article 'Cuddly Grandparent puppets axed as Wonga attempts big clean-up' taken from http://www.bbc.co.uk/news/business-28294258 © BBC (Model Paper 1 page 2);
An extract from the article 'FCA proposes payday loans cap of 0.8% per day' taken from http://www.bbc.co.uk/news/business-28305886 © BBC (Model Paper 1 page 3);
An extract from the article 'Archbishop of Canterbury 'delighted' to cut Wonga ties' http://www.bbc.co.uk/news/business-28260222 (Model Paper 1 page 3);
Exhibit 1 taken from www.openwonga.com/ (last accessed 17/05/2015) © Wonga.com (Model Paper 1 page 4);
Exhibit 2 taken from the article 'Cuddly Grandparent puppets axed as Wonga attempts big clean-up' taken from http://www.bbc.co.uk/news/business-28294258 © BBC (Model Paper 1 page 4);
Exhibit 3 taken from the article 'FCA proposes payday loans cap of 0.8% per day' taken from http://www.bbc.co.uk/news/business-28305886 © BBC (Model Paper 1 page 4);
Photo public domain — http://creativecommons.org/publicdomain/zero/1.0/deed.en (Model Paper 2 page 2);
Logo and extracts taken from http://www.marysmeals.org.uk © Mary's Meals (Model Paper 3 pages 2 to 5);
Logo and extracts taken from http://www.arnoldclark.com © Arnold Clark (Model Paper 4 pages 2 to 4);
A photograph, extract and logos for Google © Google PLC (2015 pages 2 to 5);
Image © Twin Design/Shutterstock.com (2015 page 3).

Hodder Gibson would like to thank SQA for use of any past exam questions that may have been used in model papers, whether amended or in original form.